Brian
May God bless
you always
Madge
Madge
January
2005

KEYHOLE to the KINGDOM

Glimpses of God

TRUDY MADGE

TATE PUBLISHING, LLC

Published in the United States of America

By TATE PUBLISHING, LLC

All rights reserved.
Do not duplicate without permission.

Book Design by TATE PUBLISHING, LLC.

Printed in the United States of America by

TATE PUBLISHING, LLC

127 East Trade Center Terrace

Mustang, OK 73064

(888) 361-9473

Publisher's Cataloging in Publication

Madge, Trudy

KEYHOLE TO THE KINGDOM, Trudy Madge

Originally published in Mustang,OK:TATE PUBLISHING:2004

1. Spiritual 2. General Religious

ISBN 1-9331482-4-1 $12.95 (US) $19.95 (CAN)

Copyright 2004

First Printing: November 2004

DEDICATION

My Lord and my God, Jesus Christ

> All praise be to You. You loved me and chose me before I ever knew You. Without You, I am nothing.

My husband, Ed

> You are the love of my life, my best friend, my lover. You have always believed I could do anything. You are always there for me. I thank God for you more than you will ever know.

My Children

Rob & Michelle

Ed & Tina

Grandchildren

Zachariah

Katiara & Connor

> You are the icing on the cake, the cherry on the sundae, you give my life joy, may God continue to bless and protect you forever.

My Father and Mother

> You gave me the greatest gift that parents can give their children. You loved each other. A special thank you to my mother for instilling in me at an early age a life long love of books and reading.

My sister, Valerie

> You encouraged me, pushed me, prodded me when I needed it, and discussed concepts and ideas with me for hours. You were my walking concordance. Without you, this book would never have been written.

My brothers, Ross and Allan

> You unknowingly contributed to this book and provided me with some of the inspiration. I thank you for that.

TABLE OF CONTENTS

INTRODUCTION

The book you are about to read is not one about "getting religion" but about one ordinary woman's experiences in discovering the reality of the words she wrote in a margin of her Bible when she was a young girl—*God is love*. It is a testimony of how the knowledge of God is learned in a day by day commitment to know the Truth; not by mystic or emotional experiences, sudden bursts of light or writing on the wall, but by virtue of obeying the urging of Jesus to ask, seek, and knock. This invariably results in the persistent seeker being rewarded with glimpses of God the Father, who knows His children even to the very number of hairs on their head.

The miracles—both large and small—described in this book have been witnessed by someone who has watched as the author has grown in grace and knowledge out of a life which she, herself, has described as one of "quiet desperation" into one in which she has been gifted beyond her natural abilities and given far more than she could have thought or asked. One simple, yet far reaching, decision preceded this unfolding of blessings; the decision to surrender her life and will to Jesus.

Keyhole to the Kingdom defies categorization. The author uses gravity and humour, simple logic and a little theology, and personal experience consistently backed up by God's Word. The underlying message of the book is that what God wants most is not to be entertained by us jumping through religious hoops to please Him but for us to know Him and know how much He loves us. His every commandment is for our ultimate benefit.

Valerie K. Paish

Chapter 1

THE ADVENTURE BEGINS

When our children were small we moved frequently. They were not always happy about having to leave their friends and relatives and start over in a new school. I always suggested that they consider it an adventure, an opportunity to meet new people and enjoy new experiences. That is the same way that I approach getting acquainted with God, a new and wonderful adventure.

Unfortunately, it is common among many people today, even for some church leaders, to question the authority of the Bible. The "Jesus Seminar" even goes so far as to vote on the credibility of the passages of the Bible that quote the words of Jesus. These people arbitrarily decide which portions of the Bible they will believe and which portions they will ignore. The sheer arrogance boggles the mind.

According to the New World Dictionary, Second College Edition, the definition of an Agnostic is . . . a person who believes that the human mind **cannot** know whether there is a God or an ultimate cause, or anything beyond material phenomena.

Once we get past the arguments of Creation vs. Evolution, and we decide that the only logical scenario of how we came to be here is a result of the Creator, the next important questions are:

What is God's character like?

Can anybody really know Him?

Is God simply out there somewhere watching us from a distance? as the Bette Midler song suggests.

Is He a personal God who is actually involved in the day to day affairs of His Creation?

God is simply too big, His list of attributes too long, His ways and thoughts too unlike ours, for us to be able to give a quick and easy response to these questions, but he has given us all the information we need to know Him and to discern His will for our lives in the pages of His Word.

Every occupation has a policy and procedure manual, a blueprint, a set of specs, a map, or a guide of some sort that instructs employees on what is expected of them so that they can perform their job correctly, efficiently, and in a cost-effective and ethical manner. Employees who refuse to follow or who challenge the authority of their particular manual are generally disciplined, fired, or in some cases, even criminally prosecuted.

It is inconceivable that God would have left us without a similar resource. If we do not accept the Bible as the inerrant word of God, we are left to cast blindly about. We would be trying to figure out what works in a society and in our individual lives and what doesn't, totally by trial and error. If beliefs are not based on the Bible, then what are they based on? Speculation? That doesn't sound particularly reliable. Scientific laws? It is reasonable to assume that where there is a law, there is a lawgiver. Laws do not happen in a vacuum. Besides, scientific law does not generally give any guidance at all when it comes to moral and ethical dilemmas. If everyone is left to decide what is right for themselves, then we have anarchy. What happens when someone's decision interferes with someone else's decision of what is right? Unfortunately, many grand experiments in social engineering have resulted in unspeakable suffering and misery for millions.

The evidence that we have concerning the veracity of the Bible is much too massive to be examined in-depth in this book, and it would be redundant for me to attempt it. Many good books have already been written on the subject. If you have any doubts at all, please read Know What You Believe and Know Why You Believe by Paul Little, The Signature of God and The Handwriting of God by Grant Jeffries, Don't Check Your Brain at the Door by Josh McDowell, and there are many more. There is also a website worth checking out called That Amazing Book by Terry Watkins (http:/www.av1611.0rg/amazing.html).

I have read and heard many arguments by persons who wish to point out "inaccuracies", "inconsistencies", or "errors" in the Bible. They have been concerned over so called errors such as persons they feel did not exist, dates that do not appear to be correct, and names of places that do not seem to agree with known geography. Many of these errors have already been debunked by new archaeological finds and discoveries. It is interesting to note that several of these archaeological finds have confirmed contested parts of the Bible, but no find to date has ever contradicted Scripture. Sometimes local people had a different name for someplace or someone other than the one commonly used. A misreading of the passage, or just the context in which the information is presented, sometimes gives a wrong impression of what is actually being said. Admittedly, not all of these arguments have been successfully explained. Yet most of these inconsistencies concern matters that are not crucial to the central message of Scripture.

I am not arrogant enough to believe that because I cannot explain something that it is unexplainable, or because I don't know the answer to a question there is no logical answer. I am confident that in time all will be revealed by the Holy Spirit, inerrant and complete. I use the King James Version of Scripture throughout my writing to backup the truths that I have learned—

as evidence that these truths are not just my idea. I have added emphasis in several places to stress the point I am making.

2 Timothy 3:16–17
All scripture is given by inspiration of God, and is profit-
able for doctrine, for reproof, for correction, for instruc-
tion in righteousness: That the man of God may be per-
fect, thoroughly furnished for all good works.

The Bible tells us that we cannot see God with our eyes and live.

Exodus 19:21
And the Lord said unto Moses, Go down, charge the peo-
ple, lest they break through unto the Lord to gaze, and
many of them perish.

Exodus 33:21
And he said, Thou canst not see my face; for there shall
no man see me, and live.

Human bodies are too frail and human minds are too limited to be able to comprehend His total majesty and holiness without it totally destroying us. Have you ever peered through a keyhole trying to get glimpses of what is on the other side? All we can get are glimpses of God that we can then fit together, like the pieces of a jigsaw puzzle, to get a portrait of what He is truly like.

****

When two people meet they do not immediately know everything there is to know about the other person. They get to know each other over time as their relationship grows, and they get to know each other in a variety of ways.

First, someone generally introduces them. When someone introduces you to someone, they will likely tell you something about that person. "Hi. This is Joe. He is a sports caster on the local TV station."

"I'd like you to meet Mary. She is the person who can always be counted on to drive the kids to little league." You immediately know something about Joe or Mary that you can begin to build a conversation on. If you continue the conversation, you will likely learn more about them.

Joe or Mary may invite you to their home. There you will see first hand their tastes and decorating styles, their interests and hobbies, and what they consider precious and dear to them, by the things that they possess and how they care for those things. You can also gain information about someone by talking to their friends and relatives. They may share stories of their experiences with that person that can give you valuable insights into their personalities. You might find out other fascinating details about the way they think by reading things they have written. It may be letters or cards or the valedictorian speech in their High School yearbook or a poem they may have written.

You will probably base most of your opinion about Joe or Mary on the way they relate to you. Over time you will get to know if you can count on that individual in times of crisis, if you can trust them with your secrets, if they make time to celebrate your victories with you, if they are likely to give good advice, and if they are simply fun to be around.

In the same way that you would build a relationship with Joe or Mary, you can also build a relationship with God. First, someone introduces you and gives you a place to start. Then you talk to Him in prayer. You look to His creation because the whole universe is a reflection of His personality since He is the one who designed it. He has filled it with things that He values.

Psalm 19:1
The Heavens declare the glory of God; and the firmament showeth his handiwork.

Habakkuk 2:14
For the earth shall be filled with the knowledge of the
glory of the Lord, as the waters cover the sea.

You listen and talk to other Christians regarding their experiences with Him. You read His written Word, and then you see how His Word applies in your life. You watch how He helps you deal with your sorrows and you joys. You find that you have fun in His presence and that you enjoy His company.

Chapter 2

WHEN FIRST WE MET

I grew up in a home where I was taught Christian values. We attended church and Sunday school, and my mother was a Sunday school teacher. We said Grace and bedtime prayers, and my parents were hard working and honest. They were involved in the community league, home, school, Brownies, and Cubs. I even prayed the prayer in the Gideon Bible I received in grade five, but there was something missing. I never learned about having a personal relationship with Christ. I was supposed to be good and moral. That way, I would have a better, more uncomplicated life.

As a teenager, a better, more uncomplicated life seemed pretty boring. It was the late sixties. By this time, sex, drugs, and rock and roll were what everybody was talking about. Woodstock (no, I never got there to my great regret), biker movies (Peter Fonda was my hero), and partying seemed to be the most important things. I rode with an "outlaw" biker gang one summer. I dabbled in light drug use, Ouija boards, astrology, and Spiritualism, but I always seemed to be skirting the edges of these things. At the time, I thought that was a flaw in my own personality. I recognize now that it was the Holy Spirit restraining me from total disaster. Although I tried to walk away from Him, He never walked away from me.

At sixteen, I became pregnant by my biker boyfriend. I had left home to live with him. We planned to get married, but two weeks before the wedding he got cold feet and ran off with his ex-girlfriend, so I moved back home with my parents until the baby was born. Then my son, Robert, and I moved into an apartment with my best friend. Robert's father appeared in my life—briefly—a couple of months later. When he started dating my room-mate, I decided this was too much, even for me, and I moved out once again. They got married that summer, and I didn't hear from him again until Robert turned eighteen.

His father called to say that he would like to meet him. He and his wife were divorced by then, and he was "evaluating" his life. Robert responded, "I already have a father, and I'm not looking for any more friends." We have not heard from his father since.

I got married at eighteen to a man I barely knew. At the time of our marriage my parents didn't even know his last name. He called me one night and said, "Do you want to get married in the morning?" At nine o'clock the next morning, I was downtown at the old Alberta Jasper Building.

An old man, who I think must have been the custodian, took pity on me sitting alone waiting, so he came over to keep me company. He kept me amused with stories of people who had come in to get married over the years, like the woman who came in with two men who were fist fighting. She married the winner. Then there was the man who had to go back upstairs after the blood tests because he forgot his wallet. He slipped out the back way and was never seen again.

Meanwhile, Ed had still not shown up, and these stories weren't really making me feel any more secure. Finally about 10:30, the receptionist said I had a phone call. It was Ed saying that he had to wait for the bank to open (this was in the days before ATM's), and he would be right there. He showed up at eleven o'clock. He still says that he is amazed that I waited so long. We got our blood tests and license, and at four o'clock that afternoon, we got married.

The next ten years were chaotic to say the least. Ed adopted Robert, and we had another son eight months after our marriage. I had not even realized I was pregnant again. Ed had a criminal record and was arrested again that summer for car theft. My parents put up his bail. Amazingly, he only got probation. He was an alcoholic, but I was too naive to realize it. I thought that he was just a natural born jerk. He went through a lot of jobs, got into lots of fights, and was emotionally and physically abusive. There were enough good times that I kept hoping things would get better, and I didn't know how I would manage as a single parent of two small children. My pride also had a lot to do with it. I didn't want to admit that everyone was right that said it wouldn't last.

I was an enabler. My pride kept insisting that everything was not that bad. I covered for Ed with his bosses, friends, and relatives. I held a job and paid the bills. I turned to other people for affirmation and never confronted Ed with our problems. When I got angry, I simply wouldn't talk to him at all. And I felt so very self righteous.

I began praying again. We attended church sporadically. Ed insisted that if we went to church, it had to be the denomination he had grown up with. Frankly, I found that church to be ritualistic and boring.

For a short time, we attended the denomination I had grown up with, but I quickly became disillusioned with their liberalism. Even though I had broken all the rules, I recognized that there had to be rules or else everything in life would be chaos. I did get baptized. I felt that if I did all of the "right" things my life would become better and more uncomplicated. That somehow didn't seem so bad anymore.

Ed finally hit bottom in 1982 and quit drinking. We began the painful process of trying to build a new life. The incident that precipitated this change resulted in Ed being arrested again. That was the best thing that ever happened to us. Both his lawyer and the judge who heard his case were Christians. Their handling of the case influenced Ed in ways I didn't realize at the time. He got probation again, but with conditions. One of the conditions was that he had to go to an alcohol treatment program. It was a twenty-one day program, and I attended the middle-week family program. I learned things about addictions that I never knew, and some of these things scared me. Now that Ed had quit drinking, it was not necessarily going to solve all of our problems. Drinking was just a symptom of larger problems. They told us that the void left in his life by not drinking would have to be filled with something else—a healthier way of dealing with stressors. We found that the perfect way to fill that gap was with Jesus.

I like to say that the man I was married to for the first ten years was my first husband, and the man he became when he found God again is my second husband. After all, they are two entirely different people. That is what being "born again" is all about.

I had always been an avid reader, and when I discovered Christian books I began to learn for the first time what it really meant to have a personal relationship, first with Christ and then with my husband.

We moved to Hinton the following year, and things began to change rapidly for us. Ed was offered a job as branch manager of a vacuum cleaner dealership. Our children became involved in organized sports for the first time. I got my driver's license after having my learner's permit for ten years. Things looked rosy.

Then the bottom fell out again. The company Ed worked for closed the Hinton office, putting Ed out of work. He decided to go back to school and get his high school diploma, so finances were tight. There were no jobs in Hinton; I applied everywhere and couldn't even get a job as a waitress in a bar. But God provided for us. By Christmas we couldn't even afford to go home to Edmonton for the holidays. My family all chipped in, and for our Christmas present they sent us the money for the trip. My sister and one of Ed's brothers discovered that they both had an extra turkey in their freezers and gave them to us. A friend in Hinton gave us a huge bag of various frozen vegetables from her garden. We were able to eat for the month of January.

Ed applied to go to college in Grouard and to take the Addictions Resource Worker program. He was accepted, but we had no idea where we would live. Finally, in desperation, he applied for a room in the dorm at the college, and I was going to move back to Edmonton with our children. A couple of days before he was supposed to be there, someone called us. In High Prairie, a town with a zero vacancy rate, there was a two bedroom apartment available. We took it sight unseen.

Three days after we got there I was hired as a cashier in a service station, and Ed received a student loan. A couple of months later I got a job at a bank. It was evident that God was working in our lives. What looked like setbacks were simply ways for Him to show us that He would provide for us.

After Ed completed the Addictions Resource Worker program, he registered for a two-year social worker program. Our oldest son, Robert, spent a couple of summers as a junior camp counsellor at a Christian camp. He had decided by this time that he would like to be a missionary. Our younger son, Edwin, was not interested in "religion." He wanted to be in the military when he got out of school. He joined the air cadets and later the reserves. We called them our missionary and our mercenary.

We had been in High Prairie about four years when I decided I would like to move back to the Edmonton area. There had been several deaths in the family, and my father had his first heart attack. Ed asked me to give him a couple of months to find a job. He had a job in Bon Accord within the week at a boys' ranch. That first winter, I worked in the part-time pool for the bank, working at any branch that needed temporary help. In the spring, I got on full-time at the branch in Morinville.

My father had another heart attack and passed away around this time. Thank the Lord, my sister told me later that my father had accepted Jesus as his Saviour before he died.

Robert attended North American Baptist College for a couple of years. Then he moved to Ontario to attend Sheridan College while studying Media Arts. After being involved in a messy personal relationship, Edwin Jr. also accepted Jesus as his Lord and Saviour.

Things were going well, and Ed and I decided we would like to help children who were in danger of going down some of the same paths we did. I quit my job, and we started taking in foster children. We had a therapeutic foster home for children with severe behavioural problems.

We were attending a small church in Bon Accord, but the Sunday school was tiny. Most of the children were of preschool age. The children we had were teenagers. Eventually a friend of ours suggested an Evangelical church in a neighbouring town to us. Ed agreed because we were looking for a good youth group for the foster children in our care. Strangely, when we eventually retired from foster care, we stayed with that church. It was there that I first became burdened with the need to put my faith into service and to give back something to God for all that He has done for us.

When we became involved with the Christian Motorcyclists Association in the fall of 1997, I couldn't believe how perfect it was. We had been riding a motorcycle for a few years, and this was the perfect way to combine our love of motorcycling with Christian service. Once again, God had come up with the perfect answer.

Both of our sons are Christians, and I can only thank God that they turned out well—not because of us, but in spite of us. Our oldest son is still in Ontario. His ambition is to make movies, specifically Christian movies, and he is making that dream a reality. He is married to a lovely Christian woman, Michelle. Our younger son works for Revenue Canada, but he is a Christian in spite of being a tax collector. He also has a wonderful Christian wife, Tina. We have three beautiful grandchildren, two boys and a girl. We are truly blessed.

I also thank God for the man that my husband has become and that I have finally become more like the wife that he deserves. Our relationship has grown so much over the years; it is virtually unrecognizable as the one we once had. We both admit that we were not in love when we got married. We both married for very self-centred reasons, but love has grown in direct proportion to our faith and love in Jesus.

Chapter 3

GOD IN THREE PERSONS

Perhaps one of the most difficult aspects to understand is the concept of the Trinity. The Bible tells us clearly that there is only one God, and yet three persons: Father, the Son, and the Holy Spirit. This seeming contradiction has baffled many people over the centuries.

Although they are three persons, they are in complete harmony with one another. There is never any need for a board meeting or a debate on the relative merits of an issue because they are in complete agreement with each other. They are "made of the same stuff," think the same thoughts, and come to the same conclusions.

My sister, Valerie, is my best friend and Bible study partner. She and I have spent much time talking into the wee hours of the night, reading Scripture, praying, and discerning what the Holy Spirit is teaching us. She has helped me to articulate many of the ideas that have gone into this book.

I would like to use one of her analogies to help illustrate the concept of the Trinity. I have been warned that it can be dangerous to use analogies in trying to explain the Trinity, but because this topic is one of the main stumbling blocks to many people, I feel compelled to at least try to simplify it. I realize that no analogy is perfect, and I am certainly not in any way attempting to downplay the uniqueness of the Trinity. I feel that God wants us to understand Him, at least as far as our limited imaginations allow.

If you were to fill a jug with water from the sea, that jug would contain some of the sea. If you took that jug to a lab and had the seawater analysed, you would find that it contained exactly the same elements as the water still in the sea and in exactly the same proportions. You would find that the water in your jug was exactly the same as the water in the sea in all respects.

Jesus, being fully God, was made flesh (John 1:1,14) and dwelled in a human body. We can look at God the Son and see God the Father (John14:9) because they are exactly the same in all respects.

The Holy Spirit, the third Person of the Trinity is often misunderstood. The Hebrew word for "spirit" is rauch, which means "breath." The Holy Spirit can aptly be called by the title "Breath of God." His "job" is to convict us of sin, glorify Christ, lead and teach us, and pray through us when we are unable to know how to pray for ourselves. He dwells within us.

If you ask people why Jesus came to earth most of them would say that He came to save us from our sins. While this is true, it is not the only reason. One of the primary reasons He came was to show us the Father. While we cannot look upon the Father, we can see Him by looking at His Son.

John 14:7–9

If ye had known me, ye should have known my Father also: and from henceforth ye know him, and have seen him. Philip said unto him, Lord , show us the Father, and it sufficeth us. Jesus said unto him, Have I been so long time with you, and yet hast thou not known me, Philip? He that hath seen me hath seen the Father, and how sayest thou then, Show us the Father?

Unfortunately, in our society, the word father does not always have a pleasant connotation. If one's father was hard and unyielding, unloving and unforgiving, strict and legalistic, or perhaps absent altogether, it is difficult to think of God, the Father, as loving, forgiving, longsuffering, patient, slow to anger, and always there for us.

If the first kind of father I described is what you think of when you think of God the Father, then read the book of Exodus again. Notice the number of times the people that Moses led complained. They forgot about all of the miracles God performed to rescue them from the Egyptians, claimed that God was unfair and mean, worshipped other gods, and generally were a real pain to be around—even though He unfailingly provided for all of their needs. Notice that each time their disobedience brought them a consequence, they would repent and promise to never do it again. Notice that each time they repented, God forgave them even though they invariably did do it again. It was certainly no surprise to God that they continued to sin, but His capacity and willingness to forgive was and still is without limit. His desire to bless us and lead us to the Promised Land is the one thing in this uncertain life that we can count on.

****

Some time ago my husband and I were having lunch with the Regional Evangelist of our motorcycle ministry, his wife, and another couple. He asked everyone around the table in turn, "If time, finances, pride, and fear of failure were not an issue, what would you really want to do?" When it became my turn, the answer was easy. I have always had a secret desire to write.

That posed the next questions. What to write? What do I do with what I write? The answer to the last question came to me one evening when I was reading my latest issue of the news magazine from our American parent group. On the last page was a paragraph that invited people who might like to write for the magazine to send for a copy of the guidelines for submissions. There was a catch, however. We were asked to send a self-addressed, stamped envelope with our request.

I live in Canada. Of course, a Canadian postage stamp wouldn't do any good for an item that was going to be mailed to me from the United States. I had no idea where I might acquire an American postage stamp.

One day I happened to be in our local post office. We live in a small town with a population of about one thousand, so we have a very small post office with one employee. Hardly the place one would normally look for a "specialty item." I mentioned my problem to the post mistress anyway. "Normally," she said, "you can't buy an American postage stamp in Canada. However, a friend of mine was recently travelling in the United States, and I asked her to pick up a package of postage stamps just in case somebody asked for one."

I hadn't really prayed about it, but sometimes our Father likes to give us a surprise gift. He knew that I would want an American postage stamp so He provided one. Some might say that this incident was just a coincidence. Perhaps. Remember, I didn't look high and low for the stamp. I found it in the very first place I looked, and it was an unlikely place at that. I choose to believe that the Creator of the Universe is not too busy to see that His children get what they want and need, even something as small as a postage stamp. After all, He gave us His Son without waiting for us to ask. He gave us salvation as a free gift when we didn't even know we needed it.

Don't get me wrong. We should always take our requests to Him and ask Him for the tools we need to help build His Kingdom. We need to have a relationship with Him so He knows we want His help and His gifts. At some point, we need to acknowledge that we do need salvation. Still, isn't a surprise gift from our Father sometimes really nice too?

The Gospel of John makes it very clear that Jesus, the Son, is God.

John 1:1–3
In the beginning was the Word, and the Word was with
God, and the Word was God. The same was in the begin-
ning with God. All things were made by him; and without
him was not anything made that was made.

John 1:14
And the Word was made flesh, and dwelt among us, (and
we beheld his glory, the glory as of the only begotten of
the Father,) full of grace and truth.

When Thomas called Jesus "My Lord and my God" in
John 20:28, Jesus did not deny it.

John 20:29
. . . Thomas, because thou hast seen me, thou hast
believed: blessed are they that have not seen, and yet
have believed.

Jesus said that He can forgive sin.

Mark 2:5
When Jesus saw their faith, he said unto the sick of the
palsy, Son, thy sins be forgiven thee.

This angered the scribes that heard Him because they
knew that only God can forgive sin, therefore Jesus was saying
that He is God (Mark 2: 6–7). Jesus said that He has the authority to judge the world.

Matthew 25:31–32
When the Son of man shall come in his glory, and all the
holy angels with him, then shall he sit upon the throne of
his glory: And before him shall be gathered all nations:

and he shall separate them from another, as a shepherd
divideth his sheep from the goats.

C.S. Lewis said, "A man who was just a man and said the sort of things that Jesus said wouldn't be a great moral teacher, he'd either be a lunatic — on a level with a man who says he is a poached egg — or else he'd be the devil of hell. You must make your choice . . . !"

When Jesus left us to return to Heaven, He did not leave us to muddle on alone. He promised to send a Comforter who would teach us.

John 14:16
And I will pray the Father, and he shall give you another
comforter, that he may abide with you forever.

John 14:26
But the Comforter, which is the Holy Ghost, whom the
Father will send in my name, he shall teach you all
things, and bring all things to your remembrance, what-
soever I have said unto you.

Notice that Jesus calls the Holy Spirit "Him" and not "it." The Holy Spirit is a person, not a thing. He is God in spirit form so that He can live **in** us.

Just as the Son is shining a spotlight on the Father, The Holy Spirit is shining a spotlight on the Son. He is testifying to the truth of Jesus.

John 15:26
But when the Comforter is come, whom I will send you
from the Father, even the Spirit of truth, which proceedeth
from the Father, **he shall testify of me.**

John 16:13
Howbeit when he, the Spirit of truth, is come, he will
guide you into all truth: for he will not speak of himself;

but whatsoever he shall hear, that shall he speak: and he will show you things to come.

****

One day I was listening to a ministry training tape and the instructor made the following comment, "You don't need to worry about what you are going to say to people when you are witnessing to them because it isn't you speaking, it is the Holy Spirit speaking through you. You can say Mary had a little lamb, his fleece was white as snow, and if the Holy Spirit has been working in them, they will think you said Mary's son, Jesus, is the Lamb of God, without spot, that takes away the sin of the world."

This point was demonstrated to me one time. A relative had separated from his wife, and he was dating a lot of different women. I said to him, "You should be careful about all of the women you are dating. This isn't the sixties any more."

He laughed and thought that was a cute thing to say. Some months later the subject of Christianity came up. He said, "I know you are a Christian, and I know you have been trying to save my soul for some time."

I asked him, "When did I do that?" He answered, "When you said it isn't the sixties anymore." Obviously, the Holy Spirit had been doing a lot more talking to him than I had if he took that simple comment and from it saw the need to examine the state of his soul.

Chapter 4

Is Jesus the Only Way to Salvation?

If you were to die tonight do you know where you would go? Are you absolutely sure? What is it that makes you sure?

You may think that you are going to Heaven because you've done some good things in your life. You've been good to your mother. You give money to people if they need it. You've never hurt anyone who didn't deserve it or unless you really had to. The Bible tells us that we are not saved by doing good things.

Ephesians 2:8–9
For by grace ye are saved through faith; and that not of yourselves; it is the gift of God: Not of works, lest any man should boast.

Romans 3:23
For all have sinned and come short of the glory of God.

You may think you are going to Heaven because you were baptized when you were a baby or because your family belongs to a particular denomination. Some people think that they are Christians just because North America is considered a

"Christian Culture," and they aren't worshipping strange, foreign gods. The Bible tells us that we are not saved by what our parents did for us or by where we happen to live. We must make a conscience choice to follow Jesus and make Him Lord of our life.

Romans 10:9–10
That if thou confess with thy mouth the Lord Jesus, and shalt believe in thine heart that God has raised him from the dead, thou shalt be saved. For with the heart man believeth unto righteousness, and with the mouth confession is made unto salvation.

Many people today do not like the idea that Jesus is the only way to salvation. They don't think it's fair that they must believe in Him in order to be saved. What about people who were raised in other countries where Christianity is not the accepted belief? What these people imply is that man has no choice in what he believes. Just because a person is born into a family of another faith does not mean that he cannot be lead to Christ for his salvation. In fact, this is exactly what Christ commissioned us as Christians to do.

Matthew 28:19
Go ye therefore, and teach all nations, baptizing them in the name of the Father, and of the Son, And of the Holy Ghost.

Luke 24:46–47
and said unto them, Thus it is written, and thus it behoved Christ to suffer, and to rise from the dead the third day. And that repentance and remission of sins should be preached in his name among all nations, beginning at Jerusalem.

It has been suggested that belief in Christ as the only path to salvation is a threat to peace and security and even leads to violence. While this may be interpreted as true by some, it is definitely not the way God intended it. Ephesians chapter 4 is entirely devoted to promoting peace, harmony, and speaking the truth in love when ministering to others. Jesus Himself never tried to force anyone to follow Him and had compassion for those who chose not to, as in the story of the rich young ruler (Matthew 19:16–23).

The theory of many paths to salvation fails to take into account that we, as people, do not set the criteria for salvation. God has set up the system, and we do not have authority to change it.

There is only one effective treatment for juvenile (or type 1) diabetes and that is insulin. It does not matter if some would prefer to use penicillin; it is simply a fact that penicillin will not be an effective substitute. It would be unethical for anyone with medical knowledge to agree that using penicillin is an equally valid option, just so they would not appear to be intolerant—even if the patient has a cultural history of believing that it would work and a sincere belief in its benefit. It is possible to be sincere and to be wrong.

Christ said there is only one way.

John 14:6
I am the way, the truth, and the life: no man cometh unto the Father, but by me.

1 John 5:12
He that hath the Son hath life: and he that hath not the Son of God hath not life.

1 Timothy 2:5
For there is one God, and one mediator between God and men, the man Christ Jesus.

Acts 4:12
Neither is there salvation in any other: for there is none
other name under heaven given among men, whereby we
must be saved.

Here's the bottom line. Do we believe that Christ is who He says He is? If we do not believe Him, then we are calling Him either a lunatic or a liar. If we do believe Him, then we have the duty to spread the message to everyone that we can. We do no one any favour if we spread false information about salvation even if it is wrapped in the sentiment of "pluralistic theology" or an attempt not to appear to be promoting "exclusivism."

I truly believe that our time left on earth is very short and that Christ will be returning soon to claim His bride (the Church). The signs are all around us, and I believe that we are beginning to see the fulfilment of prophecy of the end times. We need to be prepared, and we need to do all we can to insure that those around us are not left behind. That's why evangelism is so important, and why it is important that we spread the correct message. There is no time to waste.

So just what has to happen in order for someone to be saved?

Romans 3:23
"For all have sinned and come short of the glory of God."

Romans 6:23
"For the wages of sin is death . . ."

That sounds pretty hopeless, but continue reading.

" . . . but the gift of God is eternal life through Jesus Christ our Lord."

Notice it says "the gift of God." A gift is something freely given. We do not have to pay for it.

John 3:16
"for God so loved the world, that he gave his only begotten Son, that whosoever believeth in Him shall not perish, but have everlasting life."

God loves each and every one of us so much that He is not willing to leave us to suffer the eternal consequence of our own sinful lives. He sent Jesus, His Son, into the world to become a man like us, and to die on the cross paying the penalty for our sin. On the third day He was resurrected, giving us the hope of eternal life. Yet there is a catch. God has also given us a free will. We do not have to accept the gift He has given us. We can choose not to allow Him to bail us out of the mess we have made of our lives. We can choose to remain in bondage to our sin and to spend eternity separated from Him and His love.

The Bible describes Heaven for us.

John 14:2–3
"In my Father's house there are many mansions: if it were not so I would have told you. I go to prepare a place for you. And if I go and prepare a place for you, I will come again, and receive you unto myself: that where I am, there ye may be also."

Revelation 21:4
"And God shall wipe away all tears from their eyes; and there shall be no more death, neither sorrow, nor crying, neither shall there be anymore pain: for the former things are passed away."

It also gives us a description of Hell if that is what we choose.

Mark 9:44
" . . . *to go into hell, into the fire that never shall be quenched: Where their worm dieth not, and the fire is not quenched.*"

By the way, the passage about "many mansions" has often been wrongly interpreted to mean that there are many paths to salvation. No matter how many times I read it, I don't understand how it could possibly mean that. In fact, it is saying just the opposite. It is saying that one of those mansions is reserved for you—if you accept God's plan for salvation—and that Jesus Himself is preparing it for you so that you can be with Him. Read what Jesus says three verses further.

John 14:6
. . . I am the way, the truth , and the life: no man cometh unto the Father, but by me.

Jesus did not say, "I am a way" or "I am one way." He said, "I am **the** way."

There are three things we can expect to be saved from. We can be saved from the penalty of sin. The penalty for sin is death, and Jesus has already paid the penalty with His own death. We can be saved from the power of sin. When we ask Jesus into our heart, He gives us the victory over the power of sin in our life. We will be saved from the presence of sin. That is a promise for the future. As long as we live in this sinful world, we will be in the presence of sin. When we enter Heaven, sin will no longer exist.

There are four things we have to do to experience salvation. First, we have to recognize that there is a problem. Sin has separated us from God. Next, we must admit that we are powerless to fix things ourselves. Then we have to ask Christ to come into our heart and give Him permission to change us and our life. If that is what you would like to do, simply repeat the following prayer. You may personalize it by adding your own name or admitting to your specific sins.

Father God, I know that I have lived a sinful life and that I am separated from you and your love.

I know that there is nothing I can do to fix this problem by myself and that I need a Saviour.

Today I invite Jesus to come into my heart and to be the Lord of my life.

I thank you for the wonderful gift of salvation that was made possible by the sacrifice of Jesus on the cross, and I now claim the promise of eternal life made possible by the resurrection of Jesus Christ. Thank you, Lord, for your love.

I ask this in the name of the Lord Jesus Christ.

If you have said this prayer, there is one more thing you must do. You must tell someone that you have done it.

Romans 10:9
If thou shalt confess with the mouth the Lord Jesus, and believe in the heart that God has raised Him from the dead, thou shalt be saved.

Matthew 10:32–33
Whosoever therefore shall confess me before men, him will I confess also before my Father which is in Heaven. But whosoever shall deny me before men, him will I also deny before my Father which is in Heaven.

If you have prayed this prayer, please speak to someone about your decision as soon as possible, preferably a pastor of a Bible believing church.

When we go to a secular motorcycle rally for the weekend, the Christian Motorcyclist Association is sometimes asked to conduct a Sunday Service. At one of those services, the designated speaker said that non-Christians often suggest that Christianity is just a crutch. He said that he always agrees with them that they are right. He goes on to say, if you talk to someone who is crippled, they will say that it is better to get around on a crutch than not to get around at all. We are all crippled by sin. We all need the crutch of Jesus Christ.

Jesus is sometimes referred to as our Great High Priest. In the Old Testament, when the people were being led out of Egypt into the land that God promised them, they worshipped Him in the tabernacle that was carried through the desert. Later when they were settled in the land, a permanent temple was built for worship. The Ark of the Covenant of the Lord (which contained the stone tablets inscribed with the Ten Commandments) was placed in the most holy place that was separated from the sanctuary by a second veil. This is the place that was, at times, filled with God's presence.

1 Kings 8:10–11
And it came to pass, when the priests were come out of the holy place, that the cloud filled the house of the Lord. So that the priests could not stand to minister because of the cloud: for the glory of the Lord had filled the house of the Lord.

Access to the most holy place was limited to the high priest alone, and then only once each year.

Hebrews 9:6–7
Now when these things were thus ordained, the priests went always into the tabernacle, accomplishing the service of God. But into the second went the high priest alone once every year, not without blood, which he offered for himself, and the errors of the people:

The death of Jesus on the cross gives us direct access to God our Father.

Matthew 27:50–51
Jesus, when he had cried again with a loud voice, yielded
up the ghost. And, behold, the veil of the temple was rent
in twain from the top to the bottom . . .

The veil of the temple (which represents sin) no longer separates us from God. The shed blood of Jesus did what the blood of animals could never do, it cleansed us once and for all of our sins. Animal sacrifices had to be repeated each year, the one time sacrifice of Jesus is sufficient.

Hebrews 9:28
So Christ was **once** *offered to bare the sins of many..*

We no longer have to depend on human priests to make sacrifices for us because Jesus, our Great High Priest, made the perfect sacrifice for us with His own life and His own blood.

1 Peter 2:9
But ye are a chosen generation, **a royal priesthood,** *an*
holy nation, a peculiar people; that ye should show forth
the praises of him who hath called you out of darkness
into his marvellous light:

All believers can now be considered priests because we all have direct access to the throne room of God. We can make our requests and offer our praises directly to Him simply by acknowledging the finished work of Jesus on the cross. We can now, with confidence, call upon the Holy God, Creator of the Universe, King of all Creation, our Father or Abba—which can be loosely translated as "Daddy."

Chapter 5

PARADISE LOST?

There has been much debate on the issue of whether salvation, once attained, can be lost. Can we turn our backs on God? Will He turn His back on us? Can we be lured away from God? We are well aware that Christians, once saved, are still not perfect and will still sin. Even Paul struggled, listen to what he said.

Romans 7:19
For the good that I would I do not: but the evil which I would not, that I do.

Therefore we know that sin in itself will not cause us to lose our salvation.

God has told us repeatedly in His word that He will never leave us or forsake us.

1 Samuel 12:22
For the Lord will not forsake his people for his great name's sake: because it hath pleased the Lord to make you his people.

Psalm 94:14
For the Lord will not cast off his people, neither will he
forsake his inheritance.

Hebrews 13:5
. . . for he hath said, I will never leave thee,
nor forsake thee.

God has also gone to great lengths to assure us of our
salvation.

Isaiah 45:17
But Israel shall be saved in the Lord with an everlast-
ing salvation: ye shall not be ashamed nor confounded
world without end.

Isaiah 51:6
. . . but my salvation shall be forever, and my righteous-
ness shall not be abolished.

2 Thessalonians 2:13
But we are bound to give thanks always to God for you,
brethren beloved of the Lord, because God hath from the
beginning chosen you to salvation through sanctification
of the Spirit and belief of the truth.

1 Peter 1:3–5
Blessed be the God and Father of our Lord Jesus Christ,
which according to his abundant mercy hath begotten us
again to a lively hope by the resurrection of Jesus Christ
from the dead. To an inheritance incorruptible, and
undefiled, and that fadeth not away, reserved in heaven
for you. Who are kept by the power of God through faith
unto salvation ready to be revealed in the last time.

We have established that God will not forsake us and that

His salvation is everlasting. Can we then be lured away from God by Satan or can life's problems create despair enough for us to leave Him?

Joshua 1:5
There shall not any man be able to stand before thee all the days thy life; as I was with Moses, so shall I be with thee: I will not fail thee nor forsake thee.

John 10:28–29
And I give unto them eternal life; and they shall never perish, neither shall any man pluck them out of my hand. My Father, which gave them to me, is greater than all; and no man is able to pluck them out of my Father's hand.

Romans 8:35
Who shall separate us from the love of Christ? Shall tribulation, or distress, or persecution, or famine, or nakedness, or peril, or sword?

Romans 8:38–39
For I am persuaded, that neither death, nor life, nor angels, nor principalities, nor powers, nor things present, nor things to come, nor height, nor depth, nor any other creature, shall be able to separate us from the love of God, which is in Christ Jesus our Lord.

Even when we go astray, even when we are doing evil, God is not about to lose what is His. We can be assured that He will stop at nothing to get us back.

In the second chapter, I told the story of how, as a teenager, I tried to ignore God and do my own thing. He never let go. He kept after me until I had no other option but to return to His love.

Nehemiah 9:31
Nevertheless for thy great mercies' sake thou didst not
utterly consume them, nor forsake them; for thou art a
gracious and merciful God.

Luke 15:4–5
What man of you, having an hundred sheep, if he lose
one of them, doth not leave the ninety and nine in the
wilderness, and go after that which is lost, until he find
it? And when he hath found it, he layeth it on his shoul-
ders, rejoicing.

John 6:39–40
And this is the Father's will which hath sent me, that of
all which he hath given me I should lose nothing, but
should raise it up again at the last day. And this is the
will of him that sent me, that everyone which seeth the
Son, and believeth on him, may have everlasting life:
and I will raise him up at the last day.

So what are we to think when we see men and women
who have been "wonderful Christians" suddenly turn their backs
and even denounce God? When a "Christian" becomes an athe-
ist, it has to give us pause.

One of two things may be happening in this case. As
the verses in Nehemiah and Luke tell us, God is relentless. He
may still be pursuing that person. If the person has already died,
we cannot presume to know what has happened in the last few
moments of his life. He may have made his peace with God in
the end. On the other hand, there is another option. That person
may never have been saved in the first place.

Matthew 7:21–23
Not every one that saith unto me, Lord, Lord, shall enter
into the kingdom of heaven; but he that doeth the will

*of my Father which is in heaven. Many will say to me in that day, Lord, Lord, have we not prophesied in thy name? and in thy name cast out devils? and in thy name done many wonderful works? And then I will profess unto them, I **never** knew you: depart from me, ye that work iniquity.*

Matthew 13:20–21
But he that received the seed in to stony places, the same is he that heareth the word, and anon with joy receiveth it ; Yet he hath no root in himself, but dureth for awhile: for when tribulation or persecution ariseth because of the word, by and by he is offended.

Revelation 3:9
Behold, I will make them of the synagogue of Satan, which say they are Jews, and are not, but do lie; behold, I will make them to come and worship before thy feet, and to know that I have loved thee.

The Bible tells us that when we are saved, we are **sealed** by God as one of His own.

2 Corinthians 1:21–22
Now he which stablisheth us with you in Christ, and hath anointed us, is God. Who hath sealed us, and given the earnest of the Spirit in our hearts.

Ephesians 1:12–13
That we should be to the praise of his glory, who first trusted in Christ. In whom ye also trusted, after that ye heard the word of truth, the gospel of your salvation: in whom also after that ye believed, ye were sealed with that holy Spirit of promise.

To truly understand the enormity of what that means, we must go back to the Old Testament. In those days, if a king made a decree and sealed it with his ring that decree could not be changed even by the king who had decreed it.

Esther 8:8

Write ye also for the Jews, as it liketh you, in the king's name, and seal it with the king's ring: for the writing which is written in the king's name, and sealed with the king's ring, may no man reverse.

Daniel 6:12–15

Then they came near, and spake before the king concerning the king's decree; Hast thou not signed a decree, that every man that shall ask a petition of any God or man within thirty days, save of thee, O king, shall be cast into the den of lions? The king answered and said, The thing is true, according to the law of Medes and Persians, which altereth not. Then answered they and said before the king, That Daniel, which is of the children of the captivity of Judah, regardeth not thee, O king, nor the decree that thou hast signed, but maketh his petition three times a day. Then the king, when he heard these words, was sore displeased with himself, and set his heart on Daniel to deliver him: and he laboured till the going down of the sun to deliver him. Then these men assembled unto the king, and said unto the king, Know, O king, that the law of Medes and Persians is, That no decree nor statute which the king establisheth may be changed.

It would seem to be certain that if we are sealed by God as one of His own that it is an unalterable fact that can not be changed even by the One who sealed us. If we wish to be unbiased in the conclusions that we come to and do not just use Scripture that conforms to our view of the matter, there is one other point that must be taken into consideration. The Bible does tell us unequivocally that there is one sin that is unforgivable.

Matthew 12:31–32
Wherefore I say unto you, all manner of sin and blasphemy shall be forgiven unto men: but the blasphemy against the Holy Ghost shall not be forgiven unto men. And whosoever speaketh a word against the Son of man, it shall be forgiven him: but whosoever speaketh against the Holy Ghost, it shall not be forgiven him, neither in this world, neither in the world to come.

Hebrews 6:4–6
For it is impossible for those who were once enlightened, and have tasted of the heavenly gift, and were made partakers of the Holy Ghost, And have tasted the good word of God, and the powers of the world to come, If they shall fall away, to renew them again to repentance; seeing they crucify to themselves the Son of God afresh, and put him to an open shame.

Hebrews 10:26–29
For if we sin wilfully after we have received the knowledge of the truth, there remaineth no more sacrifice for sins, But a certain fearful looking for of judgement and fiery indignation, which shall devour the adversaries. He that despised Moses' law died without mercy under two or three witnesses: Of how much sorer punishment, suppose ye, shall he be thought worthy, who hath trodden under foot the Son of God, and hath counted the blood of the covenant, wherewith he was sanctified, an unholy thing, and has done despite unto the Spirit of grace?

Are these passages referring to people who have actually been saved, received the Holy Spirit, and been sealed by God, or are they referring to pseudo-Christians who have not given their lives and wills completely to Christ and been born again? Can someone who is actually filled with the Holy Spirit then blaspheme against Him? Since God is all knowing, would He actually save and seal a person who He knows is going to commit the unforgivable sin, since we have to accept Him with a sincere heart? Because no one can truly know the mind of God, these verses should be a warning to all to be vigilant in his or her faith, to take no chances with their own salvation, to flee sin at every opportunity, and to continually thank the Father, the Son, and the Holy Spirit for the gift of salvation.

Chapter 6

THE POWER OF PRAYER

I have had people tell me that they don't know how to pray and who ask me how to pray because they want to do it "right." Prayer is not a strange and mystical incantation nor is it a religious ritual or a mantra that will only "work" if we get all of the forms and words exactly right. Prayer is simply communication between us and our Father. All He wants is for us to spend time with Him and communicate with Him from our heart.

When we pray, what we are actually doing is acknowledging that we agree with God. When we confess a sin to Him, we are not telling Him something that He doesn't know. We are merely agreeing with Him that it is a sin, stating our desire to be free of that sin and thanking Him for His forgiveness. Again, when we ask for something from Him whether it is concerning our job, our family, or our health, we are not bringing something to His attention that He is unaware of. We are admitting that we need Him and giving Him permission to act in our life. God is a gentleman and does not go where He is uninvited.

Prayer also is a time to just visit with God and enjoy each other's company. Those of you who are parents are happy when your children come to see you. They tell you what is going on in their lives—even if you already know—to reminisce about memories, to discuss things that are going on around you, to celebrate and give thanks just for being a part of each other's lives.

The Bible gives us instruction in when, where, how, and to whom we should pray.

1 Thessalonians 5:17–18
Pray without ceasing. In every thing give thanks . . .

Matthew 6:5–6
And when thou prayest, thou shalt not be as the hypocrites are: for they love to pray standing in the synagogues and in the corners of the streets, that they may be seen of men. Verily I say unto you, They have their reward. But thou, when thou prayest, enter into thy closet, and when thou hast shut the door, pray to thy Father, which is in secret; and thy Father which seeth in secret shall reward thee openly.

We are told that while we aren't to pray so that others can see us and think how good we are, we are to pray **with** others.

Matthew 18:19
Again I say unto you, That if two of you shall agree on earth as touching anything that they shall ask, it shall be done for them of my Father which is in Heaven.

Matthew 6:6–15 tells us how we should pray. Throughout all of Scripture about prayer, we are told to pray to our Father who is in Heaven.

1 Timothy 2:5
For there is one God, and one mediator between God and men, the man Christ Jesus.

Contrary to what some churches teach, nowhere in Scripture are we told that it is permissible to pray to anyone except God or that anyone except Jesus can mediate on our behalf between us and God our Father. The Bible tells us several times that Jesus prayed. Since we have already established that Jesus is God, who then is He praying to? He was praying to God the Father. Although Jesus was fully God (Colossians 2:9), He submitted to the will of His Father (Luke 22:42).

****

Ed and I were at a backyard barbeque with friends one afternoon, and the hosts asked Ed to ask the blessing before we ate. It was a dreary looking day and was threatening to rain at any moment. Ed thanked God for the food and the company and then thanked Him for the beautiful day He gave us for our barbeque. Our friends laughed and suggested that maybe it was just a little presumptuous of him to suggest to God in a back-handed sort of way that He should do something about the weather, but at that moment the sun came out and it didn't rain until our afternoon was over.

The next evening when I was reading my Bible, I came across a verse that confirmed that Ed was not being presumptuous at all.

Mark 11:24
therefore I say unto you, What things soever you desire,
when you pray, believe that ye receive them, and ye shall
have them.

****

Ed and I both drove a school bus for our rural school division. Our school division is very large. Ed drove the route that picked up students for the Behaviour Modification Class. There was only one class for that particular age group so the students he picked up were from all over the division. One student lived at the far end of the division and there did not seem to be a way to fit him into the route without him having to be on the bus for upwards of two and a half hours at a time.

The school bus superintendent asked me if I would be willing to pick up little Johnny with my personal vehicle each morning and drive him to school, and they would pay my mileage. The trip from my house to his and back to the school was one hundred and twenty kilometres. I agreed to do it.

As soon as the teachers at the school found out the plan for getting little Johnny to school, the horror stories started. They told me that I would have big problems controlling little Johnny on such a long trip, especially as I would be alone with him and have to concentrate on my driving. His previous bus driver thought I was crazy even to consider doing it. Little Johnny's own mother expressed reservations. The school division had offered to pay her to drive her own child to school, and she had refused.

The first morning I started out to pick up little Johnny with a lot of trepidation. I prayed all the way to his house. I asked God to send angels to be in my van to take care of little Johnny while I drove.

It was February and very early in the morning so it was still dark. When I picked up little Johnny and started back to the school, the sun was just starting to come up. I decided that if I could get little Johnny talking maybe he wouldn't get so bored on the long trip and would behave. I pointed out the beautiful sunrise to him and commented on the pretty colours. Johnny looked at the sky and said, "I can see pink and purple and orange and I can see Jesus." I was a little stunned by his remark. I had prayed for angels, but we had gotten Jesus Himself!

The rest of the trip was pleasant but uneventful. Then God did something else just to prove that it wasn't a fluke or happenstance. We met up with Ed's school bus about ten minutes from the school. He offered to take little Johnny on the bus so that I could take a little break before starting out on my own school bus run. The minute that little Johnny got out of my van and onto the bus he erupted. He was standing on the seats, yelling, and swearing. I had neglected to ask that the angels stay with him. They had stayed with me to take our break!

The rest of the school year our trips to school went just as calmly as the first day. I never had a moments problem with little Johnny. Whenever he happened to see me at the school, he would run up and give me a hug. I continued to pray for little Johnny that year, this time that the angels would stay with him throughout his day. His behaviour steadily improved, both in the classroom and on the school bus when he had to be on it.

****

Valerie explained a concept to me that I find intriguing, to say the least. She calls it "Quantum Praying." You may remember an old television program called "Quantum Leap." The main character was able to move back and forth through time, setting things right that once went wrong. "Quantum Praying" follows a similar pattern.

She said that one day, many years ago, her daughter, Wendy, had asked her to give her a wake-up call at 9:00 the next morning because she was starting a new job and didn't have an alarm clock. Valerie was very busy that morning and totally forgot her daughter's request until about 11:00 A.M. While driving her car, Valerie immediately began praying, "Lord, I forgot to keep my promise to phone Wendy. Please wake her up at 9:00 anyway. Thank you."

Valerie called her later in the day to apologize for forgetting to call. Wendy said, "The phone did ring at exactly 9:00 and woke me up. It was a telemarketer calling." God definitely has a sense of humour. At the time that the incident happened, Valerie also was a telemarketer. Even though one telemarketer forgot to call Wendy, God had sent her another one.

There actually is a scriptural basis for this theory. When

we are in the realm of the spirit, as we are when we are praying, we are in eternity and time is not an issue. God is not in time so He can answer our prayers retroactively.

John 4:24
God is a Spirit: and they that worship him must worship
him in spirit, and in truth.

He knows what is going to happen before it happens. He knew that Valerie was going to pray for her daughter. He was able to go ahead and answer that prayer before she actually prayed it.

Mark 6:8
. . . for your Father knoweth what things ye have need
of, before ye ask him.

I am not by any means suggesting that we can change history by praying for things after the fact. What I am saying is that God knows us and what we will do so well He can anticipate our needs before we ask. When we pray all we really need to say is thank-you.

****

Too often when we pray and don't get what we have asked for, we complain that God didn't answer our prayer. We don't seem to realize that "no" and "not now" are also legitimate answers. Most parents do not give their children everything they ask for, for a variety of reasons.

Sometimes parents do not give their children what they ask for because it would not be in the child's best interest to do so. A responsible parent will say no if the thing asked for will likely do the child more harm than good, even if the child believes that they can not possibly live without that thing. Sometimes parents say "not now" if they feel the child is not old enough or mature enough to responsibly handle the thing they want. God knows even better than a human parent what will ultimately be good for us and what won't. He then answers our prayers accordingly with yes, no, or not now.

1 John 5:14–15
And this is the confidence that we have in him, that, if we ask anything according to his will , he heareth us: And if we know that he hears us, whatsoever we ask, we know that we have the petitions that we desired of him.

In Southampton, England, on April 10, 1912, there were probably people who felt that God had not answered their prayer. They wanted to leave England to go to America, the land of promise, but the ship was leaving without them. Five days later on April 15, when the news broke that the Titanic had sunk, those same people were undoubtedly very grateful that God had said no or not now. What of the people who were aboard the Titanic? The answer to that question is dealt with in the next chapter.

Chapter 7

WHY DO BAD THINGS HAPPEN TO GOOD PEOPLE?

Probably one of the most common reasons given by unbelievers to explain their unbelief is that they don't understand how a loving and kind God could allow so much misery and pain and injustice to exist in the world. What they don't understand is that it is our very unbelief, disobedience, and insistence on doing things our own way that causes some of the pain in the first place. The things that happen are not necessarily a punishment from God but the natural and logical consequences of our own foolish choices or the foolish choices of those around us. If we wish to have a free will and not merely be puppets with God pulling the strings, then we will inevitably make wrong decisions that we, and others, will have to live with.

Sometimes, as in the case of disease or accidents, the consequence does not seem to have anything to do with a choice we have made. When sin came into the world because of man's disobedience, it not only affected man, but all of creation. The world is no longer a safe and peaceful place. Now man has to deal with natural disasters, disease, bodies that are subject to decay and death, wild animals, **and other sinful people who also have a free will.** A slogan for our society could be "Freedom of Choice." The only time that we don't believe in freedom of choice is when it is someone else's choice that we find unappealing or morally repugnant. When that choice causes us pain, we ask why God would allow it. We seldom ask why God allows our own freedom of choice.

We must not forget that we also have an enemy who is seeking to destroy us. When man chose to believe Satan's lies instead of what God told him, man gave Satan permission to run rampant over him.

Genesis 3:1–5

Now the serpent was more subtle than any beast of the field which the Lord God had made. And he said unto the woman, Yea, hath God said, Ye shall not eat of every tree of the garden? And the woman said unto the serpent, We may eat of the fruit of the trees of the garden: But of the fruit of the tree which is in the midst of the garden, God hath said, Ye shall not eat of it, neither shall you touch it, lest ye die. And the serpent said unto the woman, Ye shall not surely die: for God doth know that in the day that ye eat thereof, then your eyes shall be opened, and ye shall be as gods, knowing good and evil.

It is obvious from Satan's last comment that Adam and Eve, at this point, did not know the difference between good and evil. They were therefore innocent of any wrong that they might do. Even in our modern day court system, someone must know the difference between right and wrong before they can be convicted of a crime. What Satan did when he convinced them to disobey God and eat the forbidden fruit was to rob them of their innocence. Thereafter, they would be held guilty for their transgressions because now they were aware of the difference between good and evil.

Satan told Adam and Eve three lies in the course of this conversation.

"You will not die."

"You can't trust God. He lied to you. He is unfair."

"You can be like God. You can even be God."

Nothing much has changed. These are the same three lies that Satan uses in various forms today.

The lie that we will not die has never confused the picture so much as it does today. Due to technology, the very definition of death has been obscured. When is one really dead?

When your body stops?

When your brain stops?

When they need your organs?

When you become an inconvenience to someone?

Then there is the matter of cryogenics, cloning, and the belief in reincarnation to further muddy the waters. New research into finding the "anti-aging switch" is often in the news. The lie of immortality marches on. "You will not die."

Is God completely truthful with us?

Genesis 2:17
But of the tree of the knowledge of good and evil, thou shalt not eat of it: for in the day that thou eatest thereof thou shalt surely die.

On the face of it, this statement does not seem to be completely accurate. After all, Adam and Eve did not die that very day; they went on to live and raise many children. Chapter 5 verse 5 says that Adam lived 930 years. The most common answer given to this question is, "In that day, man began to deteriorate and die physically, and in that day he did die spiritually." While I have no doubt that this answer is correct it may not be complete. The Book of Jubilees, an ancient Hebrew writing, sheds an interesting perspective on the subject. Chapter 4:29–31 . . . And at the close of the nineteenth jubilee, in the seventh week in the sixth year [930 A.M.] thereof, Adam died, and all his sons buried him in the land of his creation, and he was the first to be buried in the earth. And he lacked seventy years of one thousand years; **for one thousand years are as one day** in the testimony of the heavens and therefore it was written concerning the tree of knowledge: 'On the day that ye eat thereof ye shall die.' For this reason **he did not complete the years of this day; for he died during it.**

It is interesting to note that Methuselah (you may have heard the saying 'as old as Methuselah'), commonly thought to be have been the man that lived the longest, only lived to be 969 years old. Even he did not live out the day. While the Book of Jubilees is not considered inspired scripture by the Christian Church, the fact that "one thousand years are as a day" is confirmed in both the Old and the New Testament.

Psalm 90:4
For a thousand years in thy sight are but as yesterday when it is past, and as a watch in the night.

2 Peter 3:8
But, beloved, be not ignorant of this one thing, that one day is with the Lord as a thousand years, and a thousand years as one day.

This is an important fact to remember when we feel that God is slow to act or to answer our prayers.

A popular New Age belief is that we can all aspire to be gods (the third lie). At the very least, we belong to ourselves and have the power to influence our own destiny. In the poem, Invictus, William Earnest Henley said, "I am the master of my fate. I am the captain of my soul."

A friend of mine, Pat, put an interesting twist on Henley's quote, "Jesus is the captain of my soul. I'm just the first-mate."

There is also another reason that bad things happen that people don't often think about. Sometimes the bad things that happen are to teach us something, or they are God's way of getting our attention when nothing else seems to work. Just as often, these things happen not for our own benefit but rather for the benefit of others.

****

On September 4, 1998, a young couple was travelling on their motorcycles with their two young children. The husband was on the first bike with his five year old son and three year old daughter in the sidecar. His wife was riding her own bike just behind him.

He attempted to pass a slow moving vehicle, and the two collided. The father and his son were thrown onto the road and were struck by a truck. The little girl died in the sidecar. His wife was just behind on her bike and watched in horror as her entire family were wiped out in seconds. The incident was horrible and sad, but that wasn't the end of the story by any means.

The wife found out that she was pregnant just days after the funeral. She believes the baby was likely conceived the night before her husband died. Through the horrible months that followed, the baby growing inside of her was her reminder that her life was not over. The child was to be the link to the family that she had lost that tragic day.

She harbours no bitterness toward God, and she talks about her husband and first two children with joy and happiness as she remembers the life they had. She and her husband had both made a decision to follow Christ, and she takes comfort from that. She knows that her family is in Heaven. The new baby is a gift from God that definitely helped get her through her time of sorrow.

People who have heard her story are inspired by her faith and her strength. Other family members have mentioned that she is the one who often gives them comfort. Her tragedy is an awesome testimony to her faith in the goodness of God.

2 Corinthians 1:3–6
Blessed be God, even the Father of our Lord Jesus Christ,

the Father of mercies, and the God of all comfort. Who comforteth us in all our tribulation., that we may be able to comfort them which are in any trouble, by the comfort wherewith we ourselves are comforted by God. For as the sufferings of Christ abound in us, so our consolation also aboundeth by Christ. And whether **we** *be afflicted, it is for* **your** *consolation and salvation, which is effectual in the enduring of the same sufferings which we also suffer: or whether* **we** *be comforted, it is for* **your** *consolation and salvation.*

****

The question "Why do bad things happen to good people?" is based upon an erroneous assumption. The assumption is that there are any "good" people to begin with.

Psalm 14:2–3
The Lord looked down from heaven upon the children of men, to see if there were any that did understand, and seek God. They are all gone aside, they are all together become filthy: there is none that doeth good , no, not one.

A better question would be "Why do any good things happen to anybody?" The only reason that any good things happen is due to God's love, mercy, and grace. God is under absolutely no obligation to bless anyone.

The Book of Job explains this very clearly. Job's friends kept insisting that he must have done something wrong for God's blessings to have been withdrawn from him. Job insisted that he had not sinned and could not understand what was happening to him. All of them missed the point entirely. My own paraphrase of what God finally told Job is this: "Are you God? Are you capable of creating anything even remotely like this world and the creatures and plant life it contains? Are you able to control the forces of nature? Do you have any power at all over what the future will bring? What gives you the right to question my authority over all of creation, including you? It is my right to bless anyone I wish (even if you don't think they deserve it) and not to bless anyone I want (even if you think they do deserve it)."

God is able to see, before the fact, where any set of circumstances will lead. We do not have that ability. Sometimes what we see as cruel and unusual punishment is the very thing we need to lead us to our greatest rewards and ultimately to salvation and to a closer personal relationship with God. Imagine a small child needing a painful and frightening medical procedure to save his or her life. The child is not capable of understanding the need for his suffering, but certainly no one would fault responsible and loving parents for proceeding with the surgery in spite of the fear and confusion it may cause.

****

Valerie was celebrating her anniversary with her husband at the Crowne Plaza Hotel. She was looking out the window of their fourteenth floor room and watching the activity going on below. She could see a man standing on the corner. She noticed that she could see for blocks from her vantage point, while the man below could see only the corner that he was on. She realized that if something should happen, perhaps a lunatic driver careening down the street, she would know about it long before the man who would be totally oblivious. She also knew that if she could somehow warn the man about the impending danger **he would have to trust that she knew something that he did not know,** or he would not be willing to take an action that might protect him.

Many people believe that God's rules about morality are unfair, unrealistic, outdated, and that God just wants to spoil their fun. They do not see anything wrong with premarital or extramarital sex. They feel that recreational drinking and drugging are just harmless ways to unwind from the pressures of life. Many people feel that pornography and prostitution are "victimless crimes" and nobody is really being hurt.

God calls these actions sin because He is able to see past the facades that these people hide behind. He is able to see the devastation that these lifestyles leave in their wake. The consequences of living wild and free of moral restraint include disease, unwanted pregnancies, abortions, single parent homes, abused and neglected children, crime, poverty, self-hatred, suicide, violence, broken families, and shattered lives.

Often the cycle of sin continues to the next generation and the next. The sins of someone we care about can hurt innocent family members and friends just as much as they hurt the person who is committing them. How could a loving and merciful God **not** call these transgressions sin?

Fortunately, God is compassionate, and He is perfectly willing to forgive us when we mess up. Indeed, we are already forgiven. All we have to do is to accept that forgiveness as a gift from God and then forgive ourselves and each other. Even if we are never to cross paths again with a person who has wronged us, we must forgive them in our hearts, not just for their benefit but for our own. It has been said that anger, hatred, and bitterness, like acid, do more damage to the vessel in which they are stored in, than to the object on which they are poured.

Psalm 86:5
For thou, Lord, art good, and ready to forgive; and plenteous in mercy unto all them that call upon thee.

Mark 11:25
And when ye stand praying, forgive, if ye have aught against any: that your Father also which is in heaven may forgive your trespasses.

1 John 1:9
If we confess our sins, he is faithful and just to forgive
our sins, and to cleanse us from all unrighteousness.

I have yet to meet a person, free of an immoral lifestyle by God's grace, who regrets the change. I have never heard the testimony of a person who said, if only it were not for God, they would be able to have all the wild sex, drugs, alcohol, and partying they really wanted. Indeed, without fail, the people I have talked to have been grateful and awed by the Holy God that put their lives back together so that they could be complete and productive people. Their families are healthier and happier. In the case of my husband and myself, our own children have told us that the biggest impact in their lives was when their father quit drinking and we turned our lives over to Christ, rather than all of the hurtful things that happened in their early childhood. That alone makes all of the changes in our lives worthwhile.

Chapter 8

WHAT GOD THINKS VS. WHAT THE WORLD THINKS

For someone to really know someone else they must know how the other person thinks and what they believe about the things that really matter. Their opinion about moral and ethical issues is what makes them who they are. A person's beliefs are largely shaped by the society in which they grew up, but do the popular opinions of 21st century society line up with the truths that God has set out for us in His Word? Do most people know who God is and what He thinks about the way society views our world?

You may not think that God's viewpoint is valid in our modern world. Wasn't that book written to ancient people many thousands of years ago? How can it still be relevant?

Psalm 100:5
For the Lord is good; his mercy is everlasting; and his
truth endureth to all generations.

Psalm 111:7–8
The works of his hands are verity and judgement; all his commandments are sure. They stand fast for ever and ever, and are done in truth and uprightness.

Psalm 117:1–2
O praise the Lord, all ye nations: praise him all ye people. For his merciful kindness is great toward us: and the truth of the Lord endureth for ever. Praise ye the Lord.

When the Bible was written, did God have any idea what kind of problems we would face today?

1 Corinthians 10:13
There hath no temptation taken you but such as is common to man: but God is faithful, who will not suffer you to be tempted above that which you are able; but will with the temptation also make a way of escape, that ye may be able to bear it.

Society tells us that man is basically good. He must be taught evil. Criminals are often excused on the grounds that they had horrendous childhoods; in Canada, the "Young Offenders Act" states that children can not be held responsible for criminal activity under the age of twelve and only minimally after that. A popular piece of conventional wisdom says, "Follow your heart. It will never steer you wrong." (I wonder then why there are so many broken hearts?) Another says, "You must trust yourself." What does God's word have to say about these beliefs?

Genesis 8:21
. . . for the imagination of man's heart is evil from his youth . . .

Psalm 51:5
Behold, I was shapen in iniquity; and in sin did my mother conceive me.

Psalm 53:2–3
God looked down from heaven upon the children of men, to see if there was any that did understand, did seek God. Every one of them is gone back: they are altogether become filthy; there is none that doeth good, no, not one.

Psalm 58:3
The wicked are estranged from the womb: they go astray as soon as they are born, speaking lies.

Proverbs 28:26
He that trusteth in his own heart is a fool . . .

Ecclesiastes 7:20
For there is not a just man upon the earth, that doeth good, and sinneth not.

Jeremiah 17:9
The heart is deceitful above all things, and desperately wicked, who can know it?

Mark 7:21–23
For within, out of the heart of men, proceed evil thoughts, adulteries, fornications, murders, thefts, covetousness, wickedness, deceit, lasciviousness, an evil eye, blasphemy, pride, foolishness: all these evils come from within, and defile the man.

Self-centeredness and greed are a part of us from birth. Most parents are aware that their children don't need to be taught these traits; they need to be taught to share and to think of others before themselves.

I drove a school bus for Head Start students. These children were three and four years old. One afternoon when I was driving them home, they began to chant, "Mine! Mine! Mine!" It did not appear that they were claiming anything in particular. I finally realized that they were just practicing. Lest we forget how to claim ownership, just continue chanting "Mine!" When my sister was two years old, she saw a tea cup at the neighbours that she liked. She stole it and then hid it. When she was asked about it, she lied. She obviously knew what she had done was wrong. Even at that very young age, she hid her actions and lied about them.

The world tells us that we must trust our fellow man. It says that we can generally count on others in times of trouble. The Bible tells us a different story.

Psalm 108:12
Give us help from trouble: for vain is the help of man.

Psalm 118:8–9
It is better to trust the Lord than to put confidence in man. It is better to trust in the Lord than to put confidence in princes.

Jeremiah 17:5
Thus saith the Lord; cursed be the man that trusteth in man . . .

Micah 7:5–6
Trust ye not a friend, put your confidence not in a guide: keep the doors of thy mouth from her that lieth in thy bosom. For the son dishonoureth the father, the daughter riseth up against her mother, the daughter-in-law

against the mother-in-law; a man's enemies are the men of his own house.

Now just a moment there, you might be thinking. People can't be all that bad. People often do good things. When there is trouble or a catastrophe we often all pull together and help others. What about all of the heroes when New York and the World Trade Centre were attacked by terrorists?

The answer to those questions lies in motivation. If we are basically evil, what motivates us to do good things in spite of ourselves? The first motivation is God's Holy Spirit. The Holy Spirit is still active in our world, and the Holy Spirit often compels us to do things that are not in our nature to do. I shudder to think what we would really be like if the Holy Spirit withdrew Himself from our lives, and we were left to our own devices.

Although the enemy, Satan, would never compel us to do anything good, he sometimes tolerates good and doesn't interfere if he thinks he can twist our motivations and turn the situation to his own advantage. When someone does something heroic, particularly a non-believer, he starts whispering in their ear, See. People aren't that bad. You don't really need God to make you a decent human being.

We have invented such occasions as "Acts of Random Kindness Week" and schools have instituted "Catch Them Being Good" programs. If we are innately good, why do we need to go to these lengths to encourage people to be kind to each other for one week out of the year and to behave well in public places such as schools?

Often people will do something good for their own benefit. They do it to gain respect or status. It either makes them feel good or makes them look good. Charities, when trying to solicit your help, will make the plea, "Give to our charity. It will make you feel so good." Celebrities may do benefits for AIDS research, world hunger, or disaster relief for the good publicity and the benefits to their image. Often we give to charity or do something to help someone because we simply don't know how to say no without looking completely self-centered and uncaring.

Does all of this mean that we should live our lives in fear, doubt, suspicion, and mistrust? God never told us that we should trust others, only that we should love others in spite of it all. We must not build our lives on faith in any human being, including ourselves, to the extent that when that person inevitably lets us down we are totally devastated and destroyed by it. We must love with our eyes wide open, knowing that ultimately the only one that we can completely trust is God our Father.

Our society encourages a very selfish form of "love." We are told that we are foolish to attempt to maintain or salvage relationships, even with members of our own families such as children, spouses, siblings, and parents if these relationships are not in our own best interest, healthy for us, or if there isn't something tangible in it for us. Society sneers at the concepts of self-sacrifice, nobility, and martyrdom.

John 15:12–13
This is my commandment, That ye love one another, as I have loved you. Greater love hath no man than this, that a man lay down his life for his friends.

Galatians 4:13
For, brethren, ye have been called unto liberty; only use not liberty for an occasion to the flesh, [to sin] but by love serve one another.

Ephesians 4:32
And be ye kind one to another, forgiving one another, even as God for Christ's sake has forgiven you.

Philippians 2:3
Let nothing be done through strife or vainglory; but in

lowliness of mind let each esteem other better than ourselves.

1 John 1:1
Behold, what manner of love the Father hath bestowed
upon us, that we should be called the sons of God . . .

Another popular bit of wisdom is that we belong only
to ourselves. No one can tell us what to do with our lives or our
bodies because they are ours.

Psalm 100:3
Know ye that the Lord he is God: it is he that made us,
and not we ourselves; we are his people, and the sheep
of his pasture.

1 Corinthians 6:19–20
What? know ye not that your body is the temple
of the Holy Ghost, which is in you, which ye have of God,
and ye are not your own? For ye are bought with a price
. . .

1 Corinthians 7:4
The wife hath not power of her own body, but the hus-
band: and likewise also the husband hath not power of
his own body, but the wife.

Before our birth, so the world tells us, we are only of
value if our mother wants us. To them it doesn't matter if anyone else may want us; our father, our grandparents, other family
members, some childless couple or that God Himself has said
that He has known us and formed us and sanctified us before we
were formed in the womb (Jeremiah 1:5).

Psalm 27:10
When my father and my mother forsake me,
then the Lord shall take me up.

Our life is deemed valueless by the world if someone—a family member, a medical professional, or the legal system—has decided that we do not posses sufficient "quality of life." The world likes to tell us that we are no more important than any other form of life on this planet. This is quite a different view than the one God has of the sanctity of human life. The word "sanctity" is derived from the Greek root "hagio" meaning something or someone set apart from and apart to for some specific purpose. God, the Creator, set humans apart from all other life forms.

Genesis 1:25–28
And God made the beast of the earth after his kind, the cattle after their kind, and everything that creepeth upon the earth after his kind, and God saw that it was good. And God said, Let us make man in our image, after our likeness: and let them have dominion over the fish of the sea, and over the fowl of the air, and over the cattle, and over all the earth, and over every creeping thing that creepeth upon the earth. So God created man in his own image, in the image of God created he him, male and female created he them. And God blessed them, and God said unto them, Be fruitful, and multiply, and replenish the earth, and subdue it: and have dominion over the fish of the sea, and over the fowl of the air, and over every living thing that moveth upon the earth.

Genesis 9:1–3
And God blessed Noah and his sons, and said unto them, Be fruitful and multiply, and replenish the earth. And the fear and the dread of you shall be upon every beast of the earth, and upon the fowl of the air, upon all that moveth

upon the earth, and upon all the fishes of the sea; into your hand are they delivered. Every living thing that moveth shall be meat for you; even as the green herb have I given you all things.

God then instituted capital punishment for shedding the blood of man.

Genesis 9:5–6
And surely your blood of your lives will I require; at the hand of every beast will I require it, and at the hand of man; at the hand of every man's brother will I require the life of man. Whoso sheddeth man's blood, by man will his blood be shed: for in the image of God made he man.

When does God say that life begins, at birth or at conception?

Exodus 21:22–23
if men strive, and hurt a woman with child, so that her fruit depart from her, and yet no mischief follow: he shall surely be punished, according to the woman's husband will lay upon him; and he shall pay as the judges determine. And if any mischief follow, then thou shalt give life for life.

This passage may seem difficult to understand because of the unfamiliar wording and phrases of seventeenth century English. Simply put, it says if a pregnant woman gets between two men who are fighting and premature labour begins but there is no other injury (the baby is born alive and uninjured) then the aggressor must pay a fine. If the baby dies, then the aggressor must be dealt with **as anyone else who kills someone.**

Psalm 139:13–16
For thou hast possessed my reigns: thou hast covered me

in my mother's womb. I will praise thee; for I am fearfully and wonderfully made: marvellous are thou works; and that my soul knoweth right well. My substance was not hid from thee, when I was made in secret, and curiously wrought in the lowest parts of the earth. Thine eyes did see my substance, yet being unperfect; and in thy book all of my members were written, which in continuance were fashioned, when as yet there were none of them.

Jeremiah 1:5
Before I formed thee in the belly I knew thee; and before thou comest forth out of the womb I sanctified thee . . .

Ephesians 1:4
According as he has chosen us in him before the foundation of the world . . .

From all Biblical accounts, human life is sacred. All human life has intrinsic value, not because of developmental milestones or personal achievements, but because we were created in God's image. We have value because God wants us.

Chapter 9

GOD'S PLAN FOR OUR LIVES

A relative once said that he wasn't willing to give control of his life to Christ because he was afraid of what He would want him to do with it. He might send him somewhere he would hate like the Arctic Circle and might want him to do things he doesn't want to do. I can relate to that. After all, look at what He has asked me to do. Ride a motorcycle. Socialize with people. Camp out in the summer. Talk to bikers. Travel. Pass on the message of salvation. I truly believe that since God gives us our passions and talents anyway, we are sure to like what He wants us to do. This is not to say that we won't be stretched beyond our comfort level. Speaking in public does not come naturally to me. In school, I would never raise my hand even when I knew the answer for fear of embarrassing myself. When I first started working in an office, I refused to answer the phone until the other women ganged up on me and wouldn't answer the phone either until I did. The fact that I am now able to speak to people about Jesus is truly a gift of the Holy Spirit.

Psalm 37:23
The steps of a good man are ordered by the Lord: and he delighteth in his way.

Ephesians 1:4–5
According as he hath chosen us in him before the foun-
dation of the world, that we should be holy and without
blame before him in love: Having predestinated us unto
the adoption of children before Jesus Christ to himself,
according to the good pleasure of his will.

****

Our motorcycle trip east did not go quite as planned — at least by us. Perhaps it followed God's plan exactly. We had asked for prayer that we would have opportunities to witness and did we get opportunities!

It started when we met up with a fellow riding a sports bike in Saskatoon. He was going from Cold Lake CFB to visit his family in Manitoba. We rode with him for the rest of his trip, and because he was riding a sports bike, he had to stop frequently to stretch and unkink. So we had plenty of opportunities to talk to him.

We stopped for something to eat in Yorkton. I got up to get some salt when I heard a screech. I turned around and saw a woman hugging Ed. I can't turn my back for a moment! It turned out she was a woman he had worked with many years before. We hadn't seen her for about six years. She was headed for Winnipeg for a holiday and for some reason we just happened to be in the same place at the same time in another province. Coincidence? Maybe.

We turned south at Brandon Manitoba and headed for North Dakota. I loved North Dakota, Minnesota, and Wisconsin. They are beautiful and even smell good. The weather had been perfect. We got a few splatters of rain, but we didn't even need our rain gear except for one hour. It always seemed that the rain had just stopped right as we got somewhere.

Unfortunately, we hit a heat wave when we got to Michigan. The temperature was well over 100F, and there were warnings not to even go outside—and we were riding a motorcycle wearing black leather and black helmets! I succumbed to heat exhaustion. There was no way I could get back on the bike; I was too sick. Ed called Robert, our son, and had him meet us in Saginaw, Michigan, with his airconditioned car. He put down the back seat so I could lay down in the hatchback. We just got on the interstate when I had to have him pull over because another wave of nausea hit me. I must have looked cute hanging out the back of his car. I'm sure everyone that saw me must have thought I had done too much partying the day before since it was the fifth of July.

When we got to Mississauga, the temperature was still 45C. I still couldn't keep down any food, so Ed took me to the hospital and they gave me a shot of Gravol and Demerol. That perked me right up, and I was ready to party. Unfortunately, it was 3:00 A.M. by this time. For some reason, everybody else wanted to go to bed!

The rest of the week was wonderful, catching up with Rob, meeting some of his friends, meeting his girlfriend Michelle (she's now his wife), and her family. Michelle had never been on a motorcycle, but before the trip was over Ed had turned her into a biker. He took her mother for a ride too, and she loved it. They were both bugging Rob that he would have to get a bike (he still hasn't).

Thursday we left for Montreal for a few days. Robert and Michelle came with us in their car. Part of the time, Michelle rode with Ed so I got to visit with Rob. It started to rain as we neared Montreal, so Ed suggested that Michelle and I both ride with Robert. Ten minutes later, Ed crashed the bike. He was coming off the highway and someone had left a box of sand in the middle of the road at the bottom of the off ramp. He missed it with the bike, but the trailer he was towing caught it and jerked the bike. Ed flew off. The bike continued for about half a block before falling over. We were in a residential area, and a man in a neighbouring apartment called 911. The first emergency personnel was an ambulance supervisor. He arrived on the scene in a car. He checked Ed's injuries, and then volunteered to stay with us because his shift was ending and he spoke English. We didn't know if the police or tow truck driver would.

The tow truck finally arrived, but we had no idea where to take the bike. The highway peg had been pushed through the valve cover, and there was oil everywhere. It was about 10:30 P.M. by this time, and everything was closed.

At that moment, a fellow came around the corner and stopped to see what was going on. He was a biker and volunteered to let us take the bike to his mother's place for a few days. She lived in Mount Royal, a very exclusive area of Montreal. They even had private security guards patrolling at night.

Ed finally allowed us to take him to the hospital after he knew that his bike was safe. The closest hospital was Jewish General. Ed spent most of his time there witnessing. He told everyone how Jesus had looked after him, from making sure that he had no passenger at the time of the accident, to sending him the English speaking ambulance supervisor to help translate, to sending the biker with a place for his bike. That wasn't the end either. There was also the orderly at the hospital who phoned around to find us a motel room. Then there was the fellow in the waiting room who offered to ride the bike back to Alberta for us if we could get it fixed. Ed was too injured to ride. He also offered to fix up Ed's tattoo for him. We didn't take him up on either of those offers.

After taking x-rays, the doctor (who had only been a doctor for one week, by the way) couldn't decide if Ed had a new break in his ankle or if what he was seeing was an old break. No one else seemed to be able to tell either, so they put a cast on it just in case. When we finally got home and he saw a doctor here, and it was decided that it was just a severe sprain.

We rented a U-Haul truck, loaded the bike into it, and headed home that Saturday. The trip home was quite uneventful, but we did get one more opportunity to show God's love on the way home. We had stopped for the night, and we were getting something to eat at the motel restaurant. Ed noticed two young girls with a little boy sitting a few tables from us. They had a welfare voucher for food, but they only had enough for one sandwich between them. Ed went up to the waitress and gave her some money and told her to make sure that they got something good to eat.

He told her not to say anything until he had left. He had just climbed into the truck when one of the girls came running out. "You didn't have to do that," she said, practically in tears.

"Yes, I did," Ed answered. "Jesus told me to."

****

Can we thwart God's purposes by our disobedience when we refuse to follow the plan God has for our life? We should not be so presumptuous as to believe that we are able to thwart God's ultimate plan or His plans for someone else. If we refuse to be used by Him, God will use someone else. We will certainly be unable to benefit from the blessings He has for those who are obedient. He doesn't need us, but He graciously allows us to be a part of His wonderful eternal plan.

Esther 4:14
For if thou altogether holdest thy peace at this time, then shall their enlargement and deliverance arise to the Jews from another place; but thou and thy father's house shall be destroyed: and who knoweth whether thou art come to the kingdom for such a time as this?

In the story of Esther, God wished to use her to deliver the Jewish people from a slaughter. If she refused, He would have found another means to deliver them, but because she and her family were also Jewish, they would have missed out on the blessing of that deliverance.

I missed a perfect opportunity to witness to an unbelieving relative. Ed and I were collecting pledges for the Christian Motorcyclists Association annual fund raiser. We were speaking to a relative and explained the cause to him and said that we were looking for sponsors. This person had recently had some difficult circumstances happen in his life. He said very dejectedly, "I think I need a sponsor for my life."

Unfortunately, I let the moment pass. I should have said, "Have I got the man for you. Jesus would love to sponsor your life."

I couldn't believe afterward that I had missed such an obvious opening. I know that God will create other openings, perhaps for someone else, to lead this individual to Himself. I can't help feeling a little sad, though. I had an opportunity to be a part of such a wondrous thing as someone making a commitment to the Lord, and I failed to follow through with it. The blessings would have been enormous.

Chapter 10

STEPPING OUT IN FAITH

When the people of God step out in faith, God invariably does amazing things in response. The Book of Daniel relates two wonderful stories about people who boldly stepped out and declared their allegiance to the One True God, no questions asked. Their testimonies made an indelible impact on the unbelievers around them.

The first story is found in Daniel, chapter 3. King Nebuchadnezzar had made an image of gold and commanded that everyone must worship it. Anyone who refused was to be thrown into a fiery furnace. Some Chaldeans went to the king and reported to him that three Jews, Shadrach, Meshach, and Abed-nego, whom the king had set over the affairs of the province of Babylon, refused to worship the golden image. The king was furious and had the three brought to him. He commanded them again to worship the golden image.

Daniel 3:16–18
Shadrach, Meshach and Abed-nego answered and said to the king, O Nebuchadnezzar, we are not careful to answer thee in this matter. If it be so, our god whom we serve is able to deliver us from the burning fiery furnace, and he will deliver us out of thine hand, O king. **But if**

not, *be it known unto thee, O king, that we will* **not** *serve thy gods, nor worship the golden image which thou hast set up.*

The king was so furious that he had his men heat the furnace to seven times more than usual, and had the three young men thrown into the middle of it. The furnace was so hot that the men who threw them into it were killed, just from being close to it.

Daniel 3:24–25

Then Nebuchadnezzar the king was astonied [astonished], and rose up in haste, and spake, and said to his counsellors, Did not we cast three men bound into the midst of the fire? They answered and said unto the king, True, O king. He answered and said, Lo, I see four men loose, walking in the midst of the fire, and they have no hurt; and the form of the fourth is like the Son of God.

The three young men were called to come out of the furnace. When they did, everyone saw that they weren't hurt, their clothes were not burned, and they didn't even smell like smoke. The king's response was remarkable.

Daniel 3:28–29

Then Nebuchadnezzar spake, and said, Blessed be the God of Shadrach, Meshach and Abed-nego, who hath sent his angel, and delivered his servants that trusted in him, and have changed the king's word, and yielded their bodies, that they might not serve nor worship any god, except their own God. Therefore I make a decree, That every people, nation, and language which speak anything amiss against the God of Shadrach, Meshach, and Abed-nego, shall be cut in pieces, and their houses shall be made a dunghill: because there is no other God that can deliver after this sort.

The second story is found in Daniel chapter 6. King Darius thought so highly of Daniel that he was put in charge of the whole realm and the presidents and princes had to report to him. They were jealous and not very happy with this arrangement so they began to plot against Daniel. They knew that the best way to get at him was through his devotion to God.

Daniel 6:6–7
Then the presidents and princes assembled together to the king, and said thus unto him, King Darius, live forever. All the presidents of the kingdom, the governors, and the princes, the counsellors, and the captains, have consulted together to establish a royal statute, and to make a decree, that whosoever shall ask a petition of any God or man for thirty days, save of thee, O King, he shall be cast into the den of lions.

King Darius agreed and signed the decree. It was law at that time that a royal decree could not be changed by anyone, not even the king who had decreed it. When Daniel heard about the decree, he went to his room and without bothering to close his window began praying to God, just the way he had always done. King Darius' men were waiting for him, of course, and they went to the king immediately to tell him that Daniel had disobeyed the royal decree. The king was very upset for allowing himself to be used in this way and began trying to come up with ways to get Daniel out of the mess he was in, but the men reminded him that once a decree was made there was no way out.

Daniel 6:16
Then the king commanded, and they brought Daniel, and cast him into the den of lions. Now the king spake and said unto Daniel, Thy God whom thou servest continually, he will deliver thee.

The next morning, the king hurried to the lion's den and called out to Daniel, "Did God deliver you?"

Daniel 6:21–22
Then said Daniel unto the king, O king, live forever. My God hath sent his angel, and hath shut the lion's mouths, that they have not hurt me: forasmuch as before him innocency was found in me; and also before thee, O king, have I done no hurt.

When Daniel was brought out of the den he was unhurt. The king ordered his accusers thrown into the den and the lions devoured them.

Daniel 6:25–27
Then king Darius wrote unto all the people, nations, and languages, that dwell in all the earth; Peace be multiplied unto you. I make a decree, That in every dominion of my kingdom men tremble and fear before the God of Daniel: for he is the living God, and stedfast for ever, and his kingdom that which shall not be destroyed, and his dominion shall be even unto the end. He delivereth and rescueth, and he worketh signs and wonders in heaven and in earth, who hath delivered Daniel from the power of the lions.

****

Ed and I were on holidays with friends of ours, Perry and Jackie. Jackie was planning to spend a couple of days with her parents and invited us to come along. Her parents lived in a beautiful little town nestled in the mountains beside a lake with wonderful winding roads, perfect for bikers. The town was quite remote with the nearest larger centre being more than an hour away. We asked her parents about the town's economy, and they laughed and said that the town was almost entirely supported by the growing and selling of marijuana. A lot of hippies had congregated there in the sixties, and many had stayed.

On Sunday afternoon, we attended a local music festival that was being held in the park. There were baked goods for sale, a second hand book table where I found some interesting treasures, and we met some of the local people and listened to the music. It was a pleasant afternoon. When we walked out to the parking lot afterward, we found attached to our motorcycle, a small woven cross and a note that said:

Go forth & preach the gospel.

John 3:16
For God so loved the world that he gave his one and only
son that whosoever believes in him shall not perish but
receive life eternal.

John 3:16 Your sister in Christ Corrine
When we ride our motorcycle, Ed and I wear leather vests with a large back patch on it that says "Christian Motorcyclists Association" and the slogan "Riding for the Son." Our motorcycle also says "Christian Motorcyclists Association" on it, so it is not difficult for someone to figure out that we are Christians.

Because we were in a very small community, it didn't take much asking around to find out who Corrine was. She had already left the festival, but we were able to get directions to her place, which was right on the highway a few kilometres out of town. We decided that since we were leaving the next day, we would stop at her place on the way out of town and thank her and encourage her to keep encouraging other Christians.

The next morning, we headed in the general direction of home. When we travel, we don't tend to make too many plans about where we are going to end up. Our best trips have always been the ones where we simply go whichever way looks interesting and stay wherever we are when we get tired. We did want to make a stop at Corrine's, however.

A short time later we passed a place that looked somewhat like the instructions we had been given, and we pulled over to the side of the road. We decided that it was probably the place we had just passed, and we had a brief discussion about if we should just continue on since we had already passed it or if we wanted to turn around and go back. We decided to go back.

The young woman who opened the door for us was slightly built, seemed somewhat shy, and was visibly on edge. She certainly did not look like anyone's idea of a hero, but that is what she indeed turned out to be. We introduced ourselves, and she appeared genuinely glad to see us. We chatted for a few minutes, and then she told us an incredible story.

The morning before, Corrine had begun to have visions about an acquaintance of hers. In the visions, she could see the man sexually molesting little girls. She was, of course, very disturbed by these visions and could not get them out of her mind. She had no idea what to do about them; obviously she couldn't go to the police without evidence. If she told them she had been having visions, they would simply write her off as some kind of crackpot.

While she was worrying about it, a friend called her on the phone. As she told her friend about the visions, she was getting more and more upset. The friend suggested that Corrine should probably get out of the house for awhile and suggested that she should go to the music festival to get her mind off of it. Corrine hesitated, saying that she had very little gas in her car. However, her friend kept insisting, so she finally agreed to go.

As she was driving down the highway, her car started to sputter. She ran out of gas directly in front of the driveway of the man she had the vision about. As she was sitting there trying to figure out what she should do next, the man came out with a friend to see what the problem was. Corrine told them that she had run out of gas and the friend offered to go fill a jerry can for her. The first man walked back to his yard and began puttering around.

As Corrine sat there waiting for her gas, she heard a Voice speaking to her. You have to confront this person with the vision that you had. You must tell him to repent and ask for forgiveness. Corrine was shocked. You've got to be kidding! I can't do that!

The Voice continued to speak to her, gently urging her to confront the man. Corrine tried again, I can't.

Yes you can, the Voice insisted.

Finally, she rummaged around in her car until she found a piece of paper and wrote the following note, God knows everything and sees everything. He knows what you did with those little girls. He told me to tell you that you must repent and ask for forgiveness.

She carefully folded the note, and then shaking like a leaf, she got out of her car and put the note in his mailbox. She ran back to her car, got in, and locked the doors. She thought that since she had been obedient to God, perhaps if she tried to start her car again it would miraculously start, and she could get out of there. Unfortunately, the car was still out of gas. She was still trapped there, and she still needed this man's help.

In the meantime, the man had seen her put the note in his mailbox and went to see what it was. As he read the note, she saw him begin to pace back and forth. He stared at her car for a moment, read the note again, and continued pacing back and forth. He did not try to approach her car, but he did make an obscene gesture in her direction. After what seemed an eternity, the friend returned with the gas, filled her tank, and she was on her way.

When Corrine returned home from the music festival later that afternoon and told her husband what had happened, he was infuriated. He was angry that she had put herself in the midst of such a dangerous situation. The suggestion that the vision and the voice had been from God only served to make him angrier and to question her sanity. With no support from her husband, Corrine began to second guess herself. Were the visions and the voice really from God or a product of her own imagination? Had she really accused another person of such a horrendous crime with no evidence? Was she losing her mind?

Corrine got little or no sleep that night, tossing and turning until dawn. The next morning she didn't feel any better. She sat huddled in her living room, praying, and begging God to send her some kind of confirmation that what she had experienced was real. Just as she heard a motorcycle go past her house, she heard a very clear voice say, Have peace, Corrine. Your confirmation is on the way. She heard the motorcycle return, and moments later we knocked on her door.

We were all a little stunned by the magnitude of what we had heard, and no one really had much to say after that. A short time later, we said good-bye to Corrine and continued on our way. We hadn't gone far when Ed, Jackie, Perry, and I pulled over to the side of the road again because we all felt the need to pray.

We prayed for Corrine, that God would bless her for her obedience and protect her from retaliation. We prayed for the man in the vision to be convicted by the Holy Spirit and to seek repentance and forgiveness. We prayed for healing for the victims of this horrible crime; and we thanked God that He had allowed us to be a confirmation to Corrine to continue listening for God's guidance in her life.

****

Matthew 17:20
. . . If ye have faith as a grain of mustard seed, ye shall say unto this mountain, Remove hence to yonder place; and it shall remove; and nothing shall be impossible unto you.

Chapter 11

HEARING GOD'S VOICE

Has anyone ever told you they would believe in God if He would just appear in person? They can only believe in something they can see. "If I can't see God, how can I know He is really there?" If you think about those statements for just about a minute and a half, you will realize just how inane they really are.

Jesus Christ, who is God, appeared and people still didn't believe that He was who He said He was. He lived amongst them for thirty three years. He taught as no one had taught before, as one with authority. He performed miracles to prove Himself and still people did not believe.

Someone who is blind knows when there is someone in the room even if they can't see them. Their other senses kick into high gear to let them know. People believe in a multitude of things that they can not see. I have never "seen" electricity. I have seen the effect that it has on my life and the lives of others. I have felt its power (when I have received an electric shock), and I have even heard the sound it sometimes makes. That is enough to convince me that it is real.

I have seen the effect that God has on my life and the lives of others. I have felt his power and I have even heard his voice. That is enough to convince me that He is real.

God speaks to us in a variety of ways. He speaks to us by means of his written Word, the Bible. The stories in the Bible were written to be an example to us of how people behave and how God reacts when we behave that way.

1 Corinthians 10:11
Now all of these things happened unto them for examples;
and they are written for our admonition, upon whom the
ends of the world are come.

We may be directed by the Holy Spirit to specific passages and verses in the Bible that speak to our current situation.

****

Ed and I were witnessing and ministering to a secular motorcycle group who were into wild, drunken parties. Some of the behaviours exhibited by this group were quite outrageous. We were becoming quite close to some of the members of the group, although their behaviour made me somewhat uncomfortable. After awhile, my old insecurities began resurfacing. I wondered if I really wanted my husband spending so much time with people whose values were so very different from our own. Would these new friends possibly begin to influence him, instead of our values influencing them? That night, when I was reading my Bible, I was directed to a verse that immediately gave me peace about the whole situation.

2 Peter 2:8–9
(For that righteous man dwelling among them, in seeing and hearing, vexed his righteous soul from day to day with their unlawful deeds;) The Lord knoweth how to deliver the godly out of temptations . . .

God has spoken to some through dreams and visions. In the book of Genesis, chapters 39–41, Joseph interpreted three dreams for three people (the chief butler, the chief baker, and Pharaoh) that were messages from God. The interpretations of these dreams changed Joseph's life forever and the lives of the Egyptians and the Hebrews. In the book of Revelation, God gave John a vision of the end times, so that we would be prepared for what is to come.

Revelation 1:3
Blessed is he that readeth, and they that hear the words
of this prophecy, and keep these things that are written
therin: for the time is at hand.

God may use angels to speak to us.

Hebrews 1:14
Are they not all ministering spirits, sent forth to minister
for them who shall be the heirs of salvation?

An angel of God told both Mary and Joseph that they would have a child in Luke 1: 26–38 and Matthew 1:18–25. It was an angel that told Philip to go south in Acts 8:26 so that he could minister to the Ethiopian eunuch. In Acts 10: 1–6, an angel gave Cornelius his instructions concerning how to find Peter. And just in case you think that you have never seen an angel, remember the words found in Hebrews 13.

Hebrews 13:2
Be not forgetful to entertain strangers: for thereby some
have entertained angels unawares.

God also speaks to us through other people. The Old Testament prophets spoke God's words to God's people.

Jeremiah 1:7
But the Lord said unto me, Say not, I am a child: for thou
shall go to all that I send thee, and whatsoever I com-
mand thee thou shalt speak.

Jeremiah 1:9
Then the Lord put forth his hand, and touched my mouth.
And the Lord said unto me, Behold, I have put my words
in thy mouth.

Vine's Expository Dictionary of New Testament Words defines prophecy as follows: "Though much of Old Testament prophecy was purely predictive, see Micah 5:2 eg. And John 11:51, prophecy is not necessarily, nor even primarily, fore-telling. It is the declaration of that which cannot be known by natural means. Matthew 26:68 It is forth-telling of the will of God, whether with reference to the past, present or future. See Genesis 20:27, Deuteronomy 18:18, Revelation 10:11 &11:3. In such passages as 1 Corinthians 12:28 and Ephesians 2:20 the 'prophets' are placed after the 'apostles,' since not the proph-ets of Israel are intended, but the 'gifts' of the ascended Lord. Ephesians 4:8, 11 Acts 13:1 The purpose of their ministry was to edify, to comfort, and to encourage the believers, 1 Corinthians 14:3, while it's effect upon unbelievers was to show the secrets of a man's heart are known to God, to convict of sin and to con-strain to worship vv 24,25."

God speaks to us through Jesus.

Hebrews 1:1–2
God, Who at sundry times and in divers manners spake
in times past unto the fathers by the prophets, Hath in
these last days spoken unto us by his Son, whom he hath
appointed heir of all things, by whom also he made the
worlds;

How can we tell when we are hearing God's voice? How do we know that it is not just our own thoughts, or that it's not Satan telling us to do something that will ultimately hurt us, or that we are not just plain crazy?

John 10:4–5
And when he putteth forth his own sheep, he goeth before
them, and the sheep follow him: for they know his voice.
And a stranger will they not follow, but will flee from
him: for they know not the voice of strangers.

God's voice is never hysterically urgent saying, Come on! You have to do it right now! You'll never get another chance! Move it!

1 Kings 11–12
And, behold, the Lord passed by, and a great strong wind
rent the mountains, and brake in pieces the rocks before
the Lord; but the Lord was not in the wind: and after the
wind an earthquake; but the Lord was not in the earth-
quake; and after the earthquake a fire; but the Lord was
not in the fire: and after the fire a still small voice.

Does the message you are getting agree with Scripture? God will never tell you something that is contrary to His Word. He never contradicts Himself.

James 1:17
Every good gift and every perfect gift is from above, and
cometh down from the Father of lights, with whom there
is no variableness, neither shadow of turning.

You need to have a good working knowledge of Scripture in order to recognize if it is God speaking or an impostor. You need to actively listen for His voice. As with anyone else you will meet and get to know, the more often you hear His voice the more quickly you will come to recognize it.

God sometimes speaks to us through circumstances. When everything that is happening fits together beautifully as if by divine intervention that can be just what it is, divine intervention. There should be a caution here, however. As in a court of law, circumstantial evidence alone should never be the deciding factor when determining whether or not it is God speaking to you. Even if the circumstances seem perfect, one must still apply the above criteria.

****

I had been asked to be a part of a group who would be leading an Alpha Course (an introduction to Christianity) at the Young Offenders Centre each Tuesday evening. I told them that I would be interested but there was one difficulty. At the time, Ed and I had only one vehicle, an aging minivan. He already had a weekly commitment for Tuesday evenings. We live out of town, so it was not very convenient for someone to come all of the way out to our place to pick me up each week. The Thursday evening before the course was to begin, I told Ed that I would really like to be part of this ministry. If God wanted me to do it, He would have to work out the transportation. The next morning a friend called and asked if we would be interested in trading our minivan for, not one, but two cars! They had three children and she was pregnant again, so neither of the cars were big enough for them. God had worked out the circumstances once again.

Several months later I was to find out at least one of the reasons that God wanted me at the Young Offenders Centre—enough to give me a car. One of the boys who attended our weekly course did not really appear to be getting a lot out of it. He would always sit back in the corner, he rarely spoke, didn't ask any questions, and he never volunteered to read from the material. In spite of this, he came faithfully every week and had the best attendance of any of the boys. We (the volunteers) wondered what it was that kept bringing him back.

One night I was asked to tell the boys my testimony, what it was that brought me to the Lord. When I had finished speaking and we were cleaning up to leave, this young man came up to me and started talking to me for the first time. It soon became apparent that he knew me. I was puzzled because I truly did not recognize him.

As it turned out, he had been one of our foster children many years before and had spent a year living in our home. I had not seen him since he was six years old, and he was now seventeen, which accounted for the fact that I had not recognized him. He had known who I was from the beginning, but he had been too shy to approach me until I had opened myself up to the group. The staff told me later that they had talked to him about his time at our place to determine if this meeting would have an adverse effect on him, but he described that time to them as a positive experience in his life. He had kept coming every week to the group because there was someone there who he was familiar with and who he trusted. In the process, he was able to hear the Gospel of our Lord Jesus. He had not yet made a commitment to Jesus the last time I saw him, but I am confident that it will happen.

****

In the previous chapter, Corrine knew she was hearing from God for a variety of reasons. The message she was getting was not from her own mind. Confronting this man was not something she wanted to do. In fact, she was trying to find a way out of obeying. It was certainly not a message that Satan would want her to pass on. No one else was there. So by the process of elimination that left God. The message was not contrary to Scripture. Many people in the Bible were told to confront others with their sin. The voice she heard did not hysterically command her to do this or else. He gently and calmly, but insistently, urged her to be obedient.

The next day, like a loving father, He sent her a confirmation so that she could have peace. Corrine did not tell us if she had ever heard God speak to her before, but it is possible that she already knew His voice. In any case, I am sure she will have no trouble recognizing it the next time she hears it.

Chapter 12

WISDOM, POWER, AND LOVE

I, along with probably millions of other people, love the Rich Mullins' song Awesome God. The lines "He reigns from Heaven above, With wisdom, power and love, Our God is an awesome God," sum up beautifully the personality of God.

The definition of wisdom is "the quality of being wise, power of judging rightly and following the soundest course of action, based on knowledge, experience, understanding, etc; good judgement; sagacity."

Knowledge, simply put, means knowing the facts. Understanding or empathy is actually "getting it" or putting yourself in the other fellow's shoes. Experience gives the knowledge and understanding credibility; it's not just academic anymore. None of this is useful until we actually do something with it. Wisdom is applied knowledge, experience, and understanding.

God is the embodiment of wisdom.

Job 36:5
Behold, God is mighty, and despiseth not any: he is mighty in strength and wisdom.

Psalm 104:24
O Lord, how manifold are thy works! In wisdom thou
hast made them all: the earth is full of thy riches.

Jeremiah 10:12
He hath made the earth by his power, he hath established
the world by his wisdom, and hath stretched out the heav-
ens by his discretion.

1 Corinthians 1:24–25
But unto them which are called, Both Jews and Greeks,
Christ the power of God, and the wisdom of God. Because
the foolishness of God is wiser than men; and the weak-
ness of God is stronger than men.

The difference between the wisdom of men and the wisdom of God is clearly defined for us.

James 3:13–17
Who is wise and endued with knowledge among you?
Let him show out of a good conversation his works with
meekness of wisdom. But if you have bitter envying and
strife in your hearts, glory not, and lie not against the
truth. This wisdom descendeth not from above, but is
earthly, sensual, devilish. For where envying and strife
is, there is confusion and every evil work. But the wisdom
that comes from above is pure, then peaceable, gentle,
and easy to be entreated, full of mercy and good fruits,
without partiality, and without hypocrisy.

God is the source of all wisdom.

1 Chronicles 22:12
Only the Lord give thee wisdom and understanding ...

Ezra 7:25
And thou. Ezra, after the wisdom of thy God, that is in thine hand ...

Job 28:20–23
Whence then cometh wisdom? And where is the place of understanding? Seeing it is hid from the eyes of all living, and kept close from the fowls of the air. Destruction and death say, We have heard the fame thereof with our ears. God understandeth the way thereof, and he knoweth the place thereof.

****

We have an all powerful God. There is nothing He can **not** do; with Him **all** things are possible.

Matthew 19:26
But Jesus beheld them, and said unto them, With men this is impossible; but with God all things are possible.

Mark 9:23
Jesus said unto him, If thou canst believe, all things are possible to him that believeth.

Mark 14:36
And he said, Abba, Father, all things are possible unto thee . . .

In the first chapter of Genesis, we are told the story of Creation and how God spoke the universe into existence by the power of His Word. In Exodus 9:16, we are told about God's power against Pharaoh, arguably the most powerful and influential leader of the time. Then in Deuteronomy 4:37–38, we are told how God lead His people out of Egypt by His power. The references to God's all powerful nature go on and on in the Old Testament. Two beautiful verses say it all.

Jeremiah 32:17
Ah Lord God! Behold, thou hast made the heaven and
the earth by thy great power and stretched out arm, and
there is nothing to hard for thee.

Jeremiah 32:27
Behold, I am the Lord, the God of all flesh: is there any-
thing to hard for me?

The New Testament is just as full of references to the power of our Lord, Jesus Christ. Matthew 9:6 says that Jesus has the power to forgive sin. Mark 3:15 says that He has the power to heal and cast out demons. In Luke 8:24–25, Jesus' power over the forces of nature—the wind and the seas—is demonstrated. Luke 10:19 speaks of His power over animals and His ability to control their behaviour. John 10:18 refers to His power over life and death. John 17:2 says that He has the power to give eternal life.

Matthew 28:18
And Jesus came and spake unto them, saying, All power
is given unto me in heaven and earth.

****

Our God is first and foremost a God of Love. God's love for us is a personal love.

John 3:16
For God so loved the world, that he gave his only begot-
ten Son, that whosoever believeth in him should not per-
ish, but have everlasting life.

As I read this passage, I might think that God loves the whole world (or mankind) in general but doesn't necessarily care about me as an individual. I am simply one of the crowd, and I really don't matter that much in the whole scheme of things.

God's Word says an entirely different thing.

Luke 15:4–7

What man of you, having an hundred sheep, If he loses one of them, doth not leave the ninety and nine in the wilderness, and go after that which is lost, until he find it? And when he hath found it, he layeth it on his shoulders, rejoicing. And when he cometh home, he calleth together his friends and neighbours, saying unto them, Rejoice with me; for I have my sheep which was lost. I say unto you, that likewise joy shall be in heaven over one sinner that repenteth, more than over ninety and nine just persons, which need no repentance.

If there was a party in Heaven the day **I** repented, that sounds pretty personal to me.

2 Peter 3:9

The Lord is not slack concerning his promise, as some men count slackness; but is longsuffering to us-ward, not willing that any should perish, but that all should come to repentance.

The song Amazing Love written by Billy James Foote, always makes me humbled and grateful by God's great love. "Amazing love! How can it be, That You, my King would die for me?" In our world, it is the people who lay down their lives for king and country. It is virtually unheard of for a king, president or other head of state to knowingly and willing put his/her life on the line for their people. That is something that is unique to Jesus.

God's love for each of us is the underlying theme of the entire Bible.

Jeremiah 31:3
The Lord hath appeared of old unto me. Saying, Yea, I
have loved thee with an everlasting love; therefore with
lovingkindness have I drawn thee.

Zephaniah 3:17
The Lord thy God in the midst of thee is mighty; he will
save, he will rejoice over thee with joy: he will rest in his
love, he will joy over thee with singing.

John 15:9
As the Father hath loved me, so have I loved you: con-
tinue ye in my love.

Romans 8:35
Who will separate us from the love of Christ? . . .

1 John 4:10
Herein is love, not that we loved God, but that
he loved us, and sent his Son to be the propitiation for
our sins

Two verses demonstrate that God loves us just the way we are. We do not have to "clean up our act" **before** we can come to God.

Romans 5:8
But God commeneth his love toward us, in that, while we
were yet sinners, Christ died for us.

1 John 4:19
We love him, because he first loved us.

A fellow who I will call Bill came to acceptance of Jesus as his Lord and Saviour when he was middle-aged. He had lived a rough lifestyle in his past including heavy drinking, time in prison, an anger problem, and fist fighting.

After accepting Jesus, he was a totally changed person. His love for the Lord shone through in a very obvious way, and he never tired of sharing his testimony and the path to salvation with others. He was a loving and committed family man and friend.

Unfortunately, his zealous love for the Lord led him one day to make a terribly rash and impulsive decision. He heard someone swear and blaspheme God in a church building. He was so enraged that he unthinkingly reverted to past responses and actually pulled a knife on the person, although no one was physically hurt. Shortly thereafter he died of a heart attack.

I, as well as many of his friends, believe that in God's love and mercy, He called Bill home before something worse might happen.

Years ago I read a quote that has stuck with me ever since. I cannot remember where I read it or who said it, so I unfortunately cannot give proper credit for it, but I have never forgotten the words. "The good die young before they can be corrupted. The wicked live on in the hope that they may be redeemed."

Isaiah 57:1
The righteous perisheth, and no man layeth it to heart:
and merciful men are taken away, none considering that
the righteous is taken away from the sin to come.

We have one who loves us with a perfect, eternal love. One who wants only the best for us. One who is wise enough to know exactly what that is, and one who has unlimited power to give it to us. Isn't that everyone's dream? Who could ask for anything more?

How does this picture of a loving, merciful God fall in line with the image of a vengeful God who would cast unrepentant sinners into a fiery Hell for all of eternity? I do not believe that God would choose Hell for anyone. Yes, Hell is a very real place and there are people who will spend their eternity there, but it is not God who is dangling them over the fiery pit. There are only two places where one might spend eternity; there are no other choices. There is Heaven; there is Hell.

Matthew 25:41
Then shall he say also unto them on the left hand, Depart from me, ye cursed, into everlasting fire, prepared for the devil and his angels:

Hell was prepared for the devil and his angels. We can follow them there if we wish, but Hell was never intended for people to start with. The opportunity to spend eternity in Heaven is freely **offered** to everyone and is **available** to those who choose the only route to get there that God has provided. If God were to allow people to enter Heaven with their sinful human natures intact, Heaven would soon not be Heaven. If He allowed us to bring our pride, lusts, greed, selfish ambition, jealousies, envies, prejudices, anger and hatred, Heaven would soon be no different than earth is now. If we are not willing to lay down our human nature before we go to Heaven and allow Jesus to pay for our sin for us, God cannot allow us to enter. If we cannot enter Heaven, then Satan will get us by default. There are no other choices. There is no where else for us to be but Hell. The choice is our own. We cannot blame God for it.

When John and Mary's first son was born, they had such high hopes for him. They were certain that he would be someone special. As he grew up, they soon saw that there was something dreadfully wrong.

He was a bully with the other children in the neighbourhood. He was defiant and uncooperative at school; he was rude and used foul language with his parents. He terrorized his siblings, and he had a real mean streak with small animals. He would challenge authority at every opportunity.

John and Mary did everything they could. They took him to doctors, and he was put on medication. They took him to psychologists and counsellors and tried every technique that was suggested to try to help him control his behaviour. They set down tough boundaries with natural and logical consequences for overstepping them; they rewarded good behaviour. They reasoned with him, cajoled, even begged, and prayed for him continually, but nothing seemed to help.

When he moved past harassment and began to physically harm their younger children, John and Mary had no choice. With their hearts breaking and tears streaming down their faces, they had to tell their eldest son that he was no longer welcome in their home. The well-being of their other children had to come first.

This is much the same scenario that is played out when God tells unrepentant sinners that they cannot live in Heaven. God's heart is breaking, but His first concern must be for the well-being of all of His children.

Someone invariably asks, "What of those who have never heard of Jesus? What about people who were born before Jesus lived? It is unfair for those poor, unfortunate souls to be in Hell." People who lived before Jesus was born were still saved by faith; faith in the knowledge that they could not save themselves and faith in the promise of God to send a redeemer.

Galatians 3:6–9
Even as Abraham believed God, and it was accounted to him for righteousness. Know ye therefore that they which are of faith, the same are the children of Abraham. And the scripture, foreseeing that God would justify the heathen through faith, preached before the gospel unto

Abraham, saying In thee shall all nations be blessed.
So then they which be of faith are blessed with faithful
Abraham.

Job also recognized that there was someone who could atone for sin and defeat death even though he may not have known the details of how that would happen or who it would be.

Job 19:25–26
For I know that my redeemer liveth, and that he shall
stand at the latter day upon the earth. And though after
my skin worms destroy this body, yet in my flesh shall I
see God.

Our God is a God of wisdom, power, and love. It is therefore not beyond His capabilities to save people by faith in Jesus even when they have not had the opportunity to read the Bible or hear about Him from someone else. Acts 9 tells the story of Saul, of Tarsus, who was one of the chief persecutors of Christians—threatening, slaughtering, and imprisoning them. On the road to Damascus, Jesus revealed Himself to Saul.

Acts:9:3–7
And as he journeyed, he came near Damascus: and sud-
denly there shined round about him a light from heaven:
And he fell to the earth, and heard a voice saying unto
him, Saul, Saul, why persecutest thou me? And he said,
Who art thou, Lord? And the Lord said, I am Jesus whom
thou persecutest: it is hard to kick against the pricks.
And he trembling and astonished said, Lord, what wilt
thou have me to do? And the Lord said unto him, Arise,
and go into the city, and it shall be told thee what thou
must do.

Saul was baptized and began to preach Christ, who is the Son of God, in the synagogues. His name was changed to Paul

and he became one of the bold disciples who was himself impris-
oned and persecuted for his faith. If God could convert this man
by revealing Himself to him, is it so impossible to believe that
He could do the same for anyone else who might not have ever
had an opportunity to hear the gospel of Jesus the Christ?

Chapter 13

THE ORIGINAL
PROMISE KEEPER

Pontius Pilate posed the question, "What is truth?" People today still ask the same question, and truth is becoming increasingly difficult to discern in our society. Truth or illusion? Facts and images can so easily be manipulated by anyone with an agenda. Photographs and videos can be tampered with and sound editing can make it appear that someone has said something entirely different than how it was intended. Statistics can be interpreted to mean just about anything one wants them to mean. Opinion polls can word questions in such a way that you have little choice but to answer the way they wish you to. A popular catch phrase is that your truth and my truth can be two different things, and that there are no absolutes. Our perceptions and past experiences colour our perspective of the truth.

There is a tourist attraction in Moncton, New Brunswick, called "Magnetic Hill." You can park your car at the "bottom" of Magnetic Hill and put it in neutral, and your car will roll "up" the hill! Scientists have explained this phenomenon as an optical illusion. If the horizon cannot be seen or is not level, then we can be fooled by objects that we expect to be vertical but are not. Our sense of perspective is thrown off. The truth is that the "bottom" of the hill is really the top, but our senses are telling us just the opposite. Even when the truth is explained, we still do not really believe that what we see is not real.

There are other optical illusions in nature as well. Mirages are optical illusions, or the highway appearing to be wet on a very hot day. Early in the evening, the full moon on the horizon appears to be much larger than it does later in the evening when it is high in the sky.

Most people have seen the picture that can be a very old, witch-like woman or a lovely, young woman depending on where we focus our eyes. The idea is that where we put our focus is extremely important to what we see. If we wish to distinguish between truth and lies, and if we don't want to be misled by illusions, we must focus ourselves on the only standard by which truth can be measured.

****

The problem that most people have with truth is that they have no common standard to measure against. Cultural, geographical, and historical differences in value systems and ethics have been highlighted in recent years as communication systems, world travel, and immigration have become more prevalent. It is not uncommon for one to be in close contact with others whose belief system is totally foreign to their own. In an attempt to keep the peace between all of these diverse peoples, it has become "politically incorrect" to consider any of these varying beliefs wrong. Unfortunately, while keeping the peace, truth has become the casualty.

It is completely illogical to state that two competing view points can both be correct. If I say that there is no excuse for lying and someone else says that the ends justify the means, we cannot both be right. If you say that there should be more social programs and your friend says that there should be less, one of you must be wrong. If one of us believes that God, Heaven, and

Hell exist and one of us does not, one of us is in for a hideous surprise.

The common standard with which to measure truth is Jesus.

John 18:37
Pilate therefore said unto him, Art thou a king then?
Jesus answered, Thou sayest that I am a king. To this end
was I born, and for this cause came I into the world, that
I should bear witness unto the truth. Every one that is of
the truth heareth my voice.

Ephesians 4:20–21
But ye have not so learned Christ; If so be that ye have
heard him, and have been taught by him, as the truth is
in Jesus:

1 John 5:6
This is he that came by water and blood, even Jesus
Christ; not by water only, but by water and blood. And
it is the Spirit that beareth witness, because the Spirit is
truth.

People make promises all the time. Unfortunately, they don't always keep them. No one ever keeps 100 percent of their promises 100 percent of the time. No one except God that is. People don't keep their promises for a variety of reasons.

Sometimes circumstances conspire to keep us from keeping our promises. We promise our child we'll be at their piano recital, but the business meeting runs late. We promise to take our spouse on an extravagant vacation, but the car breaks down. Maybe the furnace quits, the roof starts to leak, and soon our savings account is depleted. We promise our aging parents that we will never put them in a nursing home, but now we have four children so there isn't enough room in our home. Other commitments make it hard to give the time and energy that it requires to care for them ourselves.

We don't keep our promises because we get a better offer. We promise friends that we'll come for dinner, but then a buddy at work gets tickets to a sold out concert for the same night. We commit ourselves to a new job the very day before we get offered the job opportunity we have always dreamed of. We promise our reliable boyfriend that we will go to the prom with him and just then Prince Charming comes along.

We don't keep our promises because we change our mind. We make a promise in the heat of the moment and don't think through the consequences of our promises until we are already committed. Sometimes, we make a promise we never intend to keep to get our own way. We justify breaking our word by saying we were just kidding. Sometimes, we just plain lie.

God alone invariably keeps His word. Circumstances can't keep Him from keeping His promises because He is in entire control of all circumstances.

Matthew 28:18
. . . All power is given unto me in heaven and earth.

God never gets a better offer and He never changes His mind.

Psalm 111:7–8
The work of his hands are verity and judgement; all his commands are sure. They stand fast for ever and ever, and are done in truth and uprightness.

God fully intends to keep His word. He doesn't kid and He doesn't lie.

Deuteronomy 32:4
He is the Rock, his work is perfect: for all His ways are

judgement: a God of truth and without iniquity, just and right is he.

John 14:6
Jesus saith unto him, I am the way, the truth, and the life: no man cometh unto the Father, but by me.

John 17:17
Sanctify them through the truth: thy word is truth.

1 John 1:5
This then is the message which we have heard of him, and declare unto you, that God is light, and in him is no darkness at all.

In Genesis 3:15, God promised that the woman's seed would bruise the head of the serpent; this promise was kept in Jesus when He defeated the power of Satan and death at the cross. In Genesis 15:18–21, God promised Abram that his descendants would inherit the land that God had given him even though he had no children at the time the promise was made. When Abram was ninety-nine years old and his wife ninety, God kept His promise to give them a child, Isaac. God promised His people that He would lead them out of Egypt and into the Promised Land. This promise was kept in the books of Exodus through Deuteronomy.

These are only a few of the many promises that God made and kept throughout both the Old and the New Testaments. They were literally fulfilled in the time that they were made. They are also pictures of what God continues to do now and through eternity. The promise of the land to Abraham was literally fulfilled as well as being a picture of our eternal inheritance of the New Jerusalem. The promise of God to lead His people out of captivity in Egypt was literally fulfilled as well as being a picture of Jesus leading us out of the captivity of sin. Each and every promise of the Bible, even though it was made to a specific person or persons, has a practical application in our own lives.

Not all of God's promises are what we might consider "positive" promises. God also made "negative" promises, promises of the consequences for disobedience and wilful sin. In Jeremiah 32: 1–5 and 26–35, God promised that Israel would be taken captive by the Babylonians because they had provoked God to wrath by setting up idols and worshipping heathen gods. This promise was kept, and the people were taken into captivity for seventy years. The book of Jeremiah is filled with hundreds of promises (prophecies) of God and their fulfilment, which were mainly promises of the negative consequences of not believing and obeying what God tells us. This book also tells us that even as God promised these consequences, He was also making provision for the forgiveness of their sins (Jeremiah 32:6–15, 37–44).

Promise Keepers is an organization of Christian men dedicated to serving God, building relationships with other Christian men, serving in their churches, and strengthening their marriages and families by obedience to God. The Promise Keepers website explains why they chose the name that they did for their group. "In Christ, God kept all the promises that He made to mankind; and our name—Promise Keepers—comes from the covenant-keeping nature of the Father. As the Psalmist says: "the Lord is faithful to all His promises . . ." and since God was the first promise keeper, He is faithful to help us keep our promises."

Chapter 14

THE ADVENTURE CONTINUES

When I was growing up, I would often hear people say, "There are two things that people shouldn't talk about, politics and religion." People don't like to talk about these two topics because they tend to be divisive. There have probably been more arguments and hard feelings over these topics than any others combined. Jesus acknowledged this fact in:

Matthew 10:32–39
Whosoever therefore shall confess me before men, him will I confess also before my Father which is in heaven. But whosoever shall deny me before men, him will I also deny before my Father which is in heaven. Think not that I come to bring peace to the earth: I come not to send peace, but a sword. For I am come to set a man at variance against his father, and the daughter against her mother, and the daughter-in-law against her mother-in-law. And a man's foes shall be they of his own household. He that loveth father or mother more than me is not worthy of me: and he that loveth son or daughter more than me is not worthy of me. And he that taketh not his cross,

and followeth after me, is not worthy of me. He that find-
eth his life shall lose it: and he that loseth his life for my
sake shall find it.

The intro to the radio show Politics and Religion, which
is broadcast by Irvin Baxter's End Times Ministries, says it very
well. "Maybe we should talk about politics and religion. Politics
determine how we will live on earth. Religion determines how
we will live forever." What could possibly be more important
than that?

Proverbs 3:5
Trust in the Lord with all thine heart; and lean not unto
thine own understanding.

It is not as difficult as we may think to get to know God
because God wants us to get to know Him. He desires to have a
close relationship with His children. That is the very reason He
created us in the beginning.

Jeremiah 29:12–13
Then shall ye call upon me, and ye shall go and pray
unto me, and I will hearken unto you. And ye shall seek
me, and find me, when ye shall search for me with all
your heart.

Matthew 7:7–8
Ask, and it shall be given you; seek, and ye shall find;
knock, and it shall be opened unto you: For everyone
who asketh receiveth; and he that seeketh findeth; and to
him that knocketh it shall be opened.

God wants to give His children their desires. We don't
have to beg because we are children of the King, and He really
wants to be generous with us.

John 14:13–14
And whatsoever ye shall ask in my name, that will I do,
that the Father may be glorified in the Son. If ye shall ask
anything in my name, I will do it.

John 15:7
If ye abide in me, and my words abide in you, ye shall ask
what ye will, and it shall be done unto you.

God wants each and every one of us to share eternity with Him.

2 Peter 3:9
The Lord . . . Is longsuffering to us-ward, not willing that
any should perish . . .

He gives us every opportunity, right up to the moment of our last breath, to repent. Remember the thief on the cross.

Luke 24:43
And Jesus said unto him, Verily I say unto thee, Today
shalt thou be with me in paradise.

Some people do not think it is fair that someone who has lived a life filled with evil and then repents should receive the same reward as someone who has spent their life in Christian service. In the parable of the workers who were all paid the same, some worked all day and others only a few hours (Matthew 20:1–16). Jesus tells us that we should not concern ourselves with what others receive. Luke 15:11–32 tells us the story of the prodigal son. His brother was upset that the younger brother was welcomed home with a party after living a lifestyle of decadence and greed. Again, we are told that we should rejoice when a sinner repents and not to feel slighted because we spent our life doing our Father's will.

Everyone who repents is given the gift of eternal life spent with God, whether or not they accept the gift early in their life or on their deathbed. There are, however, rewards for accepting the Lord's grace earlier rather than later. The sooner we accept Him, the sooner we are able to benefit from the blessings that He wishes to shower on us throughout our lifetime. There is a very real risk that we will run out of time and never get the chance to repent because sudden death overtakes us when we are not looking. It has been said that there are no atheists in fox holes. While this may be true, it has also been shown that a person facing a calamity such as a plane crash will be just as likely to curse God as he is to turn to Him in repentance. The sooner we accept him, the sooner we will have an opportunity to store up treasures and rewards in Heaven. We will also have the opportunity to hear the words that others may miss, "Well done, good and faithful servant." We will be able to look back without regret that we wasted so much time and hurt so many other people along the way.

When my husband and I go to a motorcycle rally, we like to leave plenty of time to get there. We may want to take some interesting "long cuts" or stop to talk and minister to other people along the way. The biker that leaves at the last moment loads his bike in the back of his pickup truck, and heads non-stop to the rally site still gets to attend the festivities, but he misses out on the exciting adventure of getting there. He misses out on the opportunity to qualify for some of the extra awards, such as the prize for the rider who has **ridden** the longest distance. He misses out on the opportunity of the comradery of sharing his adventures with the other bikers around the campfire. He misses out on the satisfaction of knowing that he may have been able to help some other biker along the way so that biker could also be at the rally.

****

When I was a teenager, I was sitting around with a group of friends listening to the Bob Dylan song It Ain't Me, Babe.

For those of you that are too young to remember, the song is about a young man who is saying that he doesn't measure up to the standards his girlfriend has set. What she wants is someone never weak, but always strong, to protect her and defend her, whether she is right or she is wrong, someone to open each and every door, someone who will promise never to part, someone to close his eyes for her, someone to close his heart, someone who would die for her, and more. She wants someone who will pick her up each time she falls, to gather flowers constantly, to come each time she calls, a lover for her life, and nothing more.

I wistfully told my friends that the song was describing exactly the kind of man I wanted. They all laughed and said I would never find him, because such a man does not exist. If I knew how to get in touch with those people today, I would tell them that they were wrong. I did find such a man, His name is Jesus.

****

I hope that this book has been both useful and entertaining; however we have barely scratched the surface. There is so much more to know about God, and it will probably take much of eternity to really "get it." Perhaps that is why eternity is such a very long time. The Holy Spirit gives us glimpses of understanding, but these glimpses are often impressions deep in our soul that are almost impossible to articulate. Unless the Holy Spirit has been working in someone else as well, they simply will not be able to understand.

1 Corinthians 2:13–14
Which things also we speak, not in the words which man's wisdom teacheth, but which the Holy Ghost teacheth; comparing spiritual things with spiritual. But the natural man receiveth not the things of the Spirit of God: for they are foolishness unto him: neither can he know them, because they are spiritually discerned.

And so the adventure continues.

Father, we just thank you today for your love and mercy and your grace. We thank you for sending us your Son, Jesus, to be with us and for the wonderful sacrifice He made for us at the cross. We ask that all of our friends and our loved ones will come to know You in a meaningful way, so that they can have life and have it more abundantly. We ask that You guide our walk through this life and that You will make Your will known to us, so that we may bring honour to Your name. We ask all things in Jesus name. Amen.

Let the heavens be glad, and let the earth rejoice:
and let man say among the nations,
The Lord reigneth.
Let the sea roar, and the fulness thereof:
let the fields rejoice, and all that is therein.
Then shall the trees of the wood sing out
at the presence of the Lord,
because he cometh to judge the earth.
O give thanks unto the Lord;
for he is good;
for his mercy endureth forever.
And say ye, Save us, O God of our salvation,
and gather us together, and
deliver us from the heathen,
that we may give thanks to thy holy name,
and glory in thy praise.
Blessed be the Lord God of Israel for ever and ever.
And all the people said, Amen, and praised the Lord.
1 Corinthians 16:31–36

COPYRIGHT

All Scripture references are King James Version, unless otherwise indicated.

Webster's New World Dictionary, Second College Edition, copyright 1974 by WILLIAMS COLLINS + WORLD PUBLISHING CO., INC

Mere Christianity, C.S. Lewis, copyright C. S. Lewis 1942, 1943, 1944 made and printed in Great Britain by William Collins and Sons Co. Ltd.

"Invictus" William Earnest Henley, 1849–1903 Public domain

Last paragraph of chapter 7 taken from "The Christian Association of Pregnancy Support Service's" first Volunteer Training Manual, Copyright June 1999 by the Christian Association of Pregnancy Support Services 35 Bradley Drive, Suite B, Kitchener Ontario, N2A 1K3, Canada

Vine's Expository Dictionary of New Testament Words -McDonald Publishing Co. McLean Virginia 22101, ISBN 0–917–006–03–08

"Awesome God" Rich Mullins, copyright 1988 BMG Songs, Inc (ASCAP)

"Amazing Love" written by Billy James Foote published by EMI Christian Music Publishing

The Promise Keepers website , copyright 1996–2004 by Promise Keepers

"It Ain't Me, Babe" Bob Dylan , copyright 1964, renewed 1992 Special Rider Music

Contact Trudy Madge
emadge@shaw.ca
or order more copies of this book at

TATE PUBLISHING, LLC

127 East Trade Center Terrace
Mustang, Oklahoma 73064

(888) 361 - 9473

Tate Publishing, LLC

www.tatepublishing.com